FLY YELLOW SIDE UP

Garth Wallace

All the best!
Garth

Happy Landings

Other books by Garth Wallace

Pie In The Sky
Blue Collar Pilots
Don't Call Me a Legend
Derry Air
The Flying Circus

Canadian Catalogue in Publication Data

FLY YELLOW SIDE UP

fiction, humor, aviation, bush flying

first printing, 1990
second printing, 1995
third printing, 1999

Written by Garth Wallace, 1946 -

ISBN 0-9697322-1-X

C813'.54

Cover Art: **Dave Robertson**

Written and produced in Canada

Published by: **Happy Landings**
RR # 4
Merrickville, Ontario
Canada, K0G 1N0

Tel.: 613-269-2552
Fax: 613-269-3962
Web site: www.happylanding.com
E-mail: books@happylanding.com

CONTENTS

INTRODUCTION

What was the son of a ladies' wear salesman doing in a battered old floatplane filled with dead fish and drunken passengers? I was discovering the ideal situation for a city-slicker pilot to make a fool of himself.

Being a bush pilot had appealed to me as the ultimate expression of the freedom and glory that comes with flying an airplane. It was an expectation based on ignorance. I had never piloted a floatplane. A chance bush job soon taught me the northern translation for freedom and glory—long hours and hard work flying smelly airplanes. But I survived, and in the process had the time of my life. I wouldn't have traded places with anyone.

Garth Wallace

1/ RESPECT, BUT NO MONEY

I was tortured into becoming a bush pilot. I blame Dr. Ivan, but perhaps I'm being unfair. He was just a simple neurosurgeon whose substantial income allowed him to pursue his dream of learning to fly. I was his instructor, but he did not single-handedly torment me into moving up north—that was caused by repeated exposure to a string of Dr. Ivans. I only pick on him because he was one of the worst of the ham-handed student pilots at my hometown flying school.

It was after a lesson with Dr. Ivan that I suddenly felt compelled to make a career change. I had sent him out to the airplane while I completed the necessary ritual of gulping more coffee before starting. When I went outside, Dr. Ivan was standing on the airplane's low wing trying to open the door on the left side. He was having trouble because Piper Cherokee 140s don't have a door on the left side.

He grinned sheepishly at me while his fingers continued to feel along the smooth aluminum panels for some clue to the entrance. At the same time his leather shoes were grinding into the thin paint on the wing skin. It was a simple mistake. It wasn't his fault that Piper skimped on doors, but this was his sixth lesson and he had made the same error on the first five. At the sight of him doing it again, something inside me snapped. I was ready to explode.

To maintain my outward sanity I bit down hard on my tongue before I said anything, "The door'th on the other thide, Doctor." The trick worked. The pain in my tongue displaced some of my frustration.

"Oh, yes," he replied, sliding off the wing and leaving a dent in the flap. "Haven't you told me that before?

"Yeth thir, but practith makth perfect." My voice stayed calm as I smiled falsely through clenched teeth.

"Say, I never noticed you had a speech impediment before," he said. "I have a specialist friend who could take care of that."

"Get in the airplane, doctor."

5

We went flying and I repeated lesson one, as I had on our previous five flights. I flew the Cherokee during the takeoff and climb-out westbound away from the airport, sucking on my swollen tongue. I asked Dr. Ivan a simple question to keep him occupied.

"What direction are we flying, Dr. Ivan?"

"North!"

"Are you sure? Look at the gyro compass, what does it say?"

"West? That's wrong."

Before I could suggest that the instrument was right and he was wrong, Dr. Ivan reached down and reset the gyro compass to north. It was going to be another long day.

When I met Dr. Ivan, I had been instructing student pilots for a year. During that time I had learned three things. First, an apparent contradiction existed. An individual's ability to learn to fly varied inversely to his education. It was more difficult to teach a doctor to fly than a log truck driver. It was as if the doctor's brain was already filled and there was no room for anything else. On the other hand, the vast vacancies in the log truck driver's head easily absorbed knowledge. It was too bad in a way, because doctors could ill afford the extra time for the repeated lessons.

Second, I learned that the low man on the instructing staff drew the deadwood students. Every day I flew with a procession of Dr. Ivans who tried to kill me. Third, I discovered that flying instructors earned an enormous amount of respect, but no money. Dr. Ivan always complimented my patience as I sat calmly in the right seat, while he sweated bullets trying to change the radio frequency. Unfortunately, I couldn't take respect to the bank. After working for a year, flying six days a week through all the daylight hours and often into the night, I had earned $5,375.

When I started instructing, I thought I enjoyed flying. Now I wasn't so sure. There had to be a less masochistic way to make a living, but I wasn't qualified to do anything else.

It was a good time to be looking for another flying job. The economy was rolling, and the lower-income, Greyhound-travelling public had discovered that air travel was suddenly within its budget. The Boeing 747 had just come into service and had proven that it could economically carry the population of a small town across the country in the time it took to feed them all lunch. To meet the increased demand for pilots, the major airlines seemed to be hiring any experienced flyer who could spell the word *airplane*. Many veteran flying instructors were bailing out of their teaching careers to answer the call.

I hadn't flown enough hours to satisfy the airline requirements for pilots, so my career options lay with the many vacancies rippling through the rest of the industry in the wake of the airline hiring.

That same spring, the sudden departure of a flying instructor in the northern town of Paradise had thrust the manager of a float-plane service into the market for a new pilot. He needed someone with an instructor's rating to divide his flying between student pilots, a fire patrol and some charter work. The busy but short float-plane season had just begun and he had no leads. He started calling various flying schools hoping to steal one of their instructors. When he called the school where I was working, I had just finished the lesson with Dr. Ivan and I happened to answer the phone.

In thirty seconds I wanted to be a bush pilot. The job meant some instructing, but there had to be more log truck drivers in Paradise than doctors. There was one catch; I had absolutely no floatplane experience. Surprisingly, this didn't seem to bother the man on the phone as long as I was instructor qualified. It didn't even matter that I would need to upgrade my instructor rating before teaching on my own. He asked me when I could travel there for an interview.

"I have tomorrow off, is that too soon?" I replied.

"No, tomorrow will be fine, I'll see you then, good-bye," and he hung up.

I felt like a giant weight had been lifted from my shoulders. None of my background qualified me for the raw, uninsulated life of bush flying, but at the time it never occurred to me that life held anything raw and uninsulated.

There was a hurdle to clear at home, but I had already made up my mind. As far as I was concerned, I was on my way. For the rest of the day I startled my remaining students with new-found cheerfulness, but I had trouble concentrating on the lessons as my brain was crowded with visions of winging over the clear blue lakes and lush forests of the north in a floatplane.

The hurdle at home was Susan, my wife of six months. Our marriage was currently going through the delicate transition between the honeymoon and the day-to-day discoveries of wrongly squeezed toothpaste tubes. Susan had an excellent job as a fashion buyer for a chain of ladies' wear stores. She was strictly a big-city girl, and I had no idea how she would take to the suggestion of moving up north. It didn't help that she was smarter than I was and earned more money.

That night I told her I had a job interview in Paradise the next day. She looked at me as if I had announced that I was joining the navy and said, "Forget it."

Susan was no snivelling, humble new wife. She possessed a unique balance of charm and forcefulness that carried her well in the business world, but I didn't give up.

"It's just an interview," I said. "I thought I should see what other flying jobs are available."

"What am I supposed to do here while you go off to play Paul Bunyan in Paradise?"

I could see this was going to be difficult. I put my arms around her. "You would come too. If the job looks good, we both go."

We cuddled, and I talked about living closer to nature, renting a little cottage in the woods next to an unspoiled northern lake, meeting new friends and seeing new places.

"Paradise is quite civilized," I was quick to add. "It is a good-sized town with shops and restaurants." I knew that Susan's idea of roughing it was having a backyard barbeque.

"How many fashion buyers work there?" she asked. She had a good idea of the answer.

"Probably none, but the retail executive rat race is not fun anymore, you have said that yourself. It would be a good break for you to work a simple sales job in a Paradise store. On our days off, we could enjoy swimming and waterskiing along with the tourists. It will be great fun."

Susan already knew about my blind faith in the grass being greener on the other side, but from her growing interest I sensed that she too was ready for a change.

"Well, go for the interview and we'll see. You may not get the job," she said.

The prospect of moving looked better than ever; a "we'll see" from Susan was a solid maybe. I went to Paradise.

2/ HAVE YOU EVER BEEN IN A BOAT?

Gary Pettigrew was a forty-year-old, skinny runt of a man who would need tying down in a wind. He sat hunched over his desk looking through sad eyes like an obedient dog trained by force. He seemed out of place in his role as manager of Bannister Airways in Paradise. He looked at my pilot's log book and asked a few questions about my background. His tone indicated that the instructor/pilot job was mine if I wanted it.

I did. The further north I had driven from my old flying school, the more I realized that I needed this change. If there had been any doubt in my mind, it had vanished at the sight of the floatplanes bobbing beside the dock at Bannister Airways. It was a clear, cool day in April and the pine-scented air was crisp and fresh with the promise of spring. The airplanes tugged at their lines with each wave, beckoning me to join them in the blue sky. They had settled it, I was going to be a bush pilot.

Pettigrew squirmed in his chair, trying to think of what to ask me next. It seemed to me that he should just name the salary and tell me when I could start, but I remained silent, confident that the job would be mine very soon. Then came the bomb. At that moment Clifford Bannister barged through the door like a wrecking ball and stopped in the middle of the room. He glared at me with large eyes set in a puffy, red face. Clifford Bannister was a round, loud man in his mid-fifties. His entry emphasized his position as owner and president of Bannister Airways. He turned to Pettigrew and bellowed, "My God Gary, he's a walking Supercub load!"

I was admittedly heavy for my size. Eating had been a happy and frequent part of my life, but I had never considered myself a walking load for a two-place airplane. I suppressed a childish urge to toss a comeback to Bannister like "people in glass houses shouldn't throw stones." I stared nervously at the hair growing out of his ears and said nothing. Since my meeting with the manager had been friendly to this point, I waited for Pettigrew's reaction to the owner's remark. He didn't say anything.

Ignoring any formalities, Bannister plopped himself into a chair and started asking me questions. "How much time do you have flying a DeHavilland Beaver?"

The Beaver was a Canadian-built, seven-passenger wonder of a bushplane, designed to haul huge loads out of postage-stamp lakes. I had never touched one, but it was a real pilot's airplane that I hoped to fly. Bannister owned two of them.

"None sir, I have never been in one."

"Figures," he said rolling his eyes, "I suppose you have never been in a Found either."

"I have never heard of a Found, sir," I replied truthfully.

I discovered later that a Found was a smaller airplane that wanted to grow up to be a Beaver, but didn't make it. There would be days ahead when I would wish that I had never seen a Found.

"Humph," he grunted, "do you have any Cessna One-Eighty time?"

"None, but I have two hundred hours in Cessna One-Seventy-Twos," I replied.

I wasn't doing very well. These were both four-place airplanes, but comparing the One-Seventy-Two to a demanding bushplane like the One-Eighty was like comparing a Harley-Davidson to a Honda scooter with training wheels. It didn't pacify him.

Gary Pettigrew slouched lower over his desk as Bannister's face grew redder.

"Have you ever flown a Supercub before?" His tone with this question demanded a yes.

"No sir, but I have instructed on a Citabria."

I thought I might score some badly needed points here since the two types of airplanes were similar, but by his look, I could see that he had never heard of a Citabria.

His scowl worsened and my hopes of experiencing the freedom of float flying, of skimming over the area's unspoiled lakes and trees started to sink.

"Well, how much float experience do you have?"

That was it. Pettigrew knew I had none so I couldn't lie. He had, however, invited me for the interview.

"I don't have any float time, sir."

"Well goddammit Pettigrew, what is this?" his voice rose with his bulk as he heaved himself out of the chair. Leaning towards me, he barked, "Tell me son, have you ever been in a boat?"

"Yes sir," I sputtered, "I taught sailing at a boys' camp."

"Well bully for you," he roared as he left the room.

Bannister's mood may have been spiked by the still fresh memory of the previous flying instructor. Pettigrew had told me that the pilot had taken off on a drunken joy ride one night in the company's best DeHavilland Beaver. After several low passes over Bannister's house, he had torn up the floats landing on submerged rocks. He escaped Bannister's wrath by departing town straight from the wreck.

The interview was over in less than a minute. I felt that any chance of landing this job went out the door with the pompous owner. I consoled myself with the fact there were other openings with the current instructor shortage, but I had been looking forward to flying floatplanes here.

Pettigrew's nasal voice broke the silence. After nervously checking the hall to ensure that his boss was gone, he apologized. "He comes on strong, doesn't he? Don't let his gruff manner bother you."

"That's all right," I lied. I was bitter. There was no reason to invite me to Paradise to belittle me. "Thanks for the interview anyway." As I got up to leave, I extended my hand out of courtesy and an urge to help the little man unbend himself.

"Before you go, I will outline our salary structure and arrange your starting time," he wheezed.

I was only half listening, because I was still thinking of how I should have handled Bannister's barrage. I could have mentioned the skipper's pin I had earned at the junior yacht club or shown him my Red Cross swimmer's badge. I could have lied and claimed Boeing 747 float time. It took me a minute to realize what Pettigrew was saying.

"Are you suggesting that I'm hired?" I asked.

"Yes. I might say that Mr. Bannister was a bit rough on you, but he likes to sound out our new staff before they are hired. I hope you were not offended, because I have no other candidates for the job. I'm sure you will find him a fair man to work for. Are you still interested?"

I was filled with mixed emotions. The warm prospect of being able to change jobs flooded back over me, but I was suffering from the emotional whiplash dealt to me by the owner. I didn't like being fodder for the grouch, but I recovered quickly and told Pettigrew that I would accept the position. I figured if Bannister made a habit out of ripping pieces off his staff, then I could always get drunk one night and buzz his house in a Beaver before leaving town.

3/ ME TARZAN—YOU JANE

When I returned home, I started telling Susan every detail of my day, except the outcome of the interview.

She waved me silent and asked point blank, "Did they offer you the job?"

I hesitated before answering. This was Susan the businesswoman I was talking to, and I had better make it good. I didn't think I could tell her right off that I had already taken the job.

"Yes, the manager said the job was mine."

I knew from her look that she knew I wasn't telling her everything, but she strung me along to see if I would hang myself.

"What did you tell the manager?" she asked.

"I said that I would go home and discuss it with my dear, swe-e-et wife," I replied.

And she said, "And what reason can you give your dear, sweet wife to convince her to quit her promising fashion career and move to some bushbound trading post up north?"

I hesitated again, trying to anticipate her reaction to the truth. She was still smiling so I said, "I could tell my dear, sweet wife that I took the job."

"YAA-HOO!" she yelled and jumped on me, giving me a big hug. "I was hoping you would."

"But I can call him back and decline," I said quickly. "If you don't want to move . . . . What did you say?"

"I said that I like the thought of playing Jane to your flying Tarzan of the Pines. I'm glad you got the job. Read my lips, Apeman. When do we move?"

Apparently she had been warming up to the idea since I had first mentioned it. Promising career or not, the competitive fashion world had been wearing her down. Susan was ready for a change.

"Just remember you said that we could rent a little cottage in the woods beside a picturesque lake."

We spent the next week talking up the good life to be found living in the vacation paradise of Paradise.

I suppose minimum quitting notice is two weeks, but in the avia-

12

tion industry, nobody is hired until he is needed yesterday. This is particularly true at flying schools, where staff have left in as little time as it takes the pilot to clear the door after receiving the right phone call. I gave my boss a week.

Our plan was for me to go on ahead, get started in the new job and find a place to live. Susan gave her boss a month's notice and would stay to settle our affairs, before following with the furniture. She was looking forward to enjoying our new surroundings with some time off before finding a job.

Before I left, I read a book on float flying and one on the Super-cub. I was determined to make a better impression on the pilots at Paradise than I had made on Clifford Bannister. I even practised tying knots. During my last week at work, I took a renewed interest in flying. I pretended that the airplane tires were now floats and I made them caress the pavement with barely a chirp on landing, as if they were kissing the water on a glassy lake.

4/ EVER SEE PEACOCKS FLY?

Bannister Airways did not fit the public image of a bush operation. It was too civilized. The floatplane complex lay on the waterfront near the foot of Main Street. It was only a short walk to several banks, shops and restaurants in Paradise. But it didn't bother me that it wouldn't be real bush flying. Living in tents and cooking on open fires were not what attracted me to the north. It was the float-planes, the freedom of going anywhere there was water and the variety of jobs associated with bush work. The fact that I could eat in restaurants and sleep in a warm bed was a bonus.

I pulled my old Volkswagen Beetle into the parking lot beside the modern four-room office building. Three of the company's float-planes sat at their moorings not far away. They were waiting for me in the warm spring sun. I felt that I had made the right decision to come here. I knew I could do a good job. It was a confidence born out of ignorance.

In the office, Beverly, the young receptionist, gave me a smile that revealed a wad of gum big enough to stop a train.

"Hi. I'm the new pilot," I said, trying to sound cool.

"Welcome to Bannister Airways," she said. Beverly had a pleasant, slinky voice that revealed nothing of her jaw's workload. "Gary is expecting you."

Our conversation brought Pettigrew from his office. He said that he was pleased to see me, but he seemed nervous.

"I'll take you to the pilot shack and introduce you to Henry Elroy, our chief pilot."

He led the way through the door, strutting like a little man who wanted to be big. The pilot shack was behind the main office. It was a ramshackle old building used as a lounge by the Airways pilots and shared with the delivery men for Bannister Propane who worked next door.

Henry Elroy was a tall, lean, country hick in his mid-forties who wore a perpetual grin. His "aw shucks" smile, plaid shirt and green work pants made him appear more like a hardware store clerk than a pilot. I eventually learned that Henry was a friendly, downhome guy who enjoyed his uncomplicated life at the Airways. At our first meeting I was intimidated by the experienced look of his deeply tanned and wrinkled face. I was afraid of how this oldtimer would react to his green replacement flying instructor. As my new boss, Henry was to check me out in one of the Supercubs and introduce me to float flying.

Pettigrew withdrew hastily, leaving us to get acquainted.

"You're the new instructor fella," Henry said it more as a statement than a question.

"Yes sir," I replied.

"Who died?"

"Pardon me sir?"

Pointing to my tie and still grinning he said, "The only time I ever wore one of them things was for a funeral; felt like a duck out of water. Makes you look like a snake oil salesman. Passengers might get nervous if you dress like you've never been in a floatplane before."

"Sorry sir," I said. Strike one; I took the tie off.

"That's okay young fella. Now I guess I'm s'posed to check you out on the Cub. How much float experience do you have?"

I was about to answer when I realized that Gary Pettigrew had not told Henry that he had hired a pilot to teach float flying who had never before been on pontoons. I summoned some confidence and replied, "I have no float experience, but I read a book all about it."

His grin fell to the floor. He dropped his gaze and said nothing. At the time I didn't know that Henry was deathly afraid of riding in an airplane as a passenger. He tolerated brief checkouts with the staff, but he hated letting them fly while he was in the plane. I discovered later that the fear was well founded from previous experience. My lack of float time meant that Henry was sentenced to a minimum of two hours in the back seat of the Supercub while I learned float flying. Strike two.

During the silence he was probably contemplating some horrible slow death for Pettigrew. He rubbed his jaw as if to make it work. After a few awkward moments, he looked up and said, "Well let's see your book." A bit of his smile was starting to grow back on his face.

I pulled the new volume from my bag and handed it to him. Henry just held it unopened and looked at me kindly. "If we took it down to the bay, do you s'pose it would float?"

I was too nervous to see the humour. I didn't know what to say. Henry finally laughed at his own joke.

"Sit down young fella, we have a lot of work to do." His face was back to full grin. My transition from big-city flying instructor to bush pilot was starting, and I was learning that I could relax around

15

Henry.

We sat in the ancient stuffed chairs of the pilot's shack while Henry talked and I listened. He began by outlining the company regulations in a way I am sure did not appear in any manual. He drew heavily from a private stock of backwoods maxims.

On weather minimums: "Don't fly when the birds are walking. If you can't see where you're going, don't go."

On aircraft loading: "A greedy bee makes more sweat and less honey. The ideal big load is two small ones. Two small loads are easier to fly and make twice as much money."

On tight situations: "If you land in a spot that's too small to get out of, it's too late to ask."

On damage: "If you bend an airplane, stay put. If you don't come back from a trip, I'll come and get you. If you fly a bent airplane, don't come back 'cause you're fired."

On air regulations: "Illegal is a sick bird. If it's not safe, don't do it."

On the manager: "Let sleeping weasels lie."

On the owner: "Don't bite the bear that feeds you."

The Henry Rules made sense. I discovered later that any pilot not following them would encounter the barnacle side of Henry. Never one to get angry, he would corner the offender in the pilot's shack and talk him into submission. He would block the only exit and recount his flying experiences in painful detail for hours. Like water torture, this safety monologue would wear down the captive. All the pilots saw this side of Henry at one time or other. With the sun going down, each of us wondered if we would ever see food or hear silence again. We would agree to everything Henry preached, right or wrong, just hoping he was on his last parable. He would not quit until he had decided that the offender would toe the line.

The lengthy dialogue I was encountering now was Henry's method of prolonging the time before flying with me. He talked about the ins and outs of float flying and some specifics about the airplane. I didn't tell him that I had read a Supercub book, thinking he would suggest we throw it into the air to see if it would fly. Keen as I was, I started to suffer the consequences of my five-hour drive that morning. While Henry discussed the finer points of step taxiing, I concentrated on the hardening lumps in my chair, trying to stay awake.

Henry took the cue when I started nodding off and he moved us down to the waterfront. The water was high that spring and the occasional wave washed over the dock. Henry hit me with one of his classic hick expressions: "Watch your step, the dock's slicker than snot on a doorknob."

"Yes sir." I replied. I liked this woodsy character.

Henry stood on the dock and told me what to check on the pre-flight inspection. The Supercub was a development of the original Piper Cub that had made William Piper famous in the 1930s. The 1958 version that I was checking was still a two-place airplane built with welded steel tubes and covered with fabric. The engine had been updated from the original 50 horsepower to a whopping 150 horsepower, giving it the name Supercub. The larger engine and the airplane's light weight earned it a reputation as a good bush plane, capable of working in and out of small lakes.

Externally the airplane was a flying study of maximum drag. There were numerous struts, control cables, brass turnbuckles and bracing wires exposed to the slipstream. The airplane's overall out-of-date appearance was not helped by its paint scheme. The same one was used on everything Bannister owned. The top half was school bus yellow and the bottom was fire engine red. The two colours were divided straight down the middle as if the airplane had been dipped like an Easter egg. The only visual breaks were the aircraft registration on the tail and small lettering under the pilot's window. I stepped closer to read it. Applied clumsily with a grade school stencil was "Fly Yellow Side Up." I smiled to myself, but said nothing.

My first chance to really make a fool of myself came when I checked each float compartment for water by pumping them out. I had trouble working the plastic bilge pump while perched precariously on the curved top of the rocking floats in my leather dress shoes. I stopped frequently to grab onto something to keep from falling in. I began to appreciate all the airplane's protruding struts and bracing wires. I managed to stay out of the bay, but I realized that I had been stupid to wear my good clothes.

Henry told me to crawl on my hands and knees across the oily spreader bar under the engine to pump out the other float. Then he said, "Ever see peacocks fly?"

It took me a minute to realize that he was referring to the way I was dressed. "No sir, I haven't."

"Neither have I," he said.

Then he had me climb into the pilot's seat to familiarize myself with the cockpit, while the airplane was still tied to the dock. Structural tubes criss-crossed the cabin and exposed control wires ran along the wooden floor. Space was limited. The two occupants sat bobsled style with the rear passenger's legs running beside the pilot's seat in the front. The interior smelled of a mixture of gasoline and old fish guts. I think discomfort was built in purposely to give passengers the impression they were roughing it. I was soon to learn that the pilot's seat was really a plywood torture device disguised by a thin layer of foam padding covered in plastic.

The instrument panel was nearly naked. As the airplane rocked on the small waves at the dock, the airspeed indicator read a steady eighty knots, the altimeter fluctuated one hundred feet up and down and the faded compass spun drunkenly on worn pivots. I mentioned these to Henry while he was installing a second control stick in the back seat.

He was still grinning as he answered me patiently, "Don't worry. This airplane is as slow as a groom going to a shotgun wedding. Fixing that speed indicator won't make it go any faster. If you want to know your height, look down. For direction, we follow the lakes and rivers and as long as I've been here, they've never changed."

There were no VOR or ADF radio navigation aids. It occurred to me that I had better learn to be a seat-of-the-pants flyer like Henry or I was going to be in trouble.

I could see the controls were simpler than in the airplanes I had been flying. Instead of a wheel, there was a stick growing out of the floor, the elevator trim control looked suspiciously like a 1950s Chevrolet window crank and there were still heel brakes installed on the floor from the airplane's previous days on wheels. Otherwise, there wasn't much. No key, just flip the magneto switches, punch the starter and go. But I still had to untie the airplane. Henry climbed into the back seat and let me do everything in a sink-or-swim approach to float flying.

I learned that the airplane drifts away as soon as it is untied. I managed to jump on board before it went too far, and then there was a mad scramble to climb in and start the engine before we drifted onto the rocks. Next I learned that floatplanes move whenever their propellors are turning. No amount of heel braking or loud "whoas" will stop them. Then I discovered that a slow-moving Supercub with the water rudders still retracted has the turning response of a large cruise ship. With liberal body English and a little luck, I managed to miss the dock ahead and make for the safety of open water. When I had a chance to glance back at Henry, he was still grinning.

"Quick to learn, quick to burn," he shouted over the engine noise coming in the open door. I think the old pilots' motto was meant to make me feel better. I counted myself lucky that my stumbling was still entertaining him.

Henry obviously wasn't in a hurry to fly. He instructed me to taxi around on the water to gain a feel for the airplane on floats. I used the time to mentally review the three distinct stages of the float takeoff as described in the book. During the initial or displacement stage, I remembered that I was to hold the stick back and wait for a bow wave to build up under the front of the floats. Then, as I felt the nose of the floats rise on the wave into the plowing stage, I was supposed to ease forward on the stick. The down elevator would force the rear of the floats out of the water onto the "step" for the planing stage. Once there, the book said to pull the stick back to find the right amount of nose-up attitude that would allow the airplane to accelerate on the step and fly into the air. In the book there was a picture of a shiny new Cessna gliding along on the step with the pilot waving at the camera.

When Henry gave the word, I was ready, I thought. The book didn't mention the unnerving, uninsulated roar or the bone-jarring vibration of full power in an old bush plane. Nor did it say anything about the spray thrown up by the propellor, momentarily obliterating all forward view. I did remember to hold the stick back, but while I was trying to feel for the bow wave building under the floats, the airplane pulled itself out of its own spray and into the air. We were flying, and I was still waiting for the second stage of the takeoff.

The Supercub's power-to-weight ratio was beyond anything written in the book, and the airplane had happily hauled itself right into the air on a curving takeoff from the displacement stage with all the noise and fury of its 150 horsepower.

I could feel Henry's pressure on the other stick ease the nose down to build up speed. We were now flying ninety degrees to our original direction and straight for the yellow and red oil storage tanks on the nearby shore. BANNISTER HOME HEATING filled the windshield. I had forgotten to counteract the Supercub's considerable torque with rudder, but Henry was still on the controls, and we turned up the bay.

I was sure that I was not impressing Henry one bit. I hazarded a look in his direction. The grin was real flat, but a trace of it was still there. Conversation over the engine noise was impossible, so he gestured for me to retake control. As preplanned, I flew south to practise some turns, slow flight and stalls. The manoeuvres gave me the chance to learn the feel of the airplane. I was surprised how easily the Supercub flew for such an old design. It was a dream; it seemed to anticipate my every move. I would think about turning and it would turn. On the other hand, I found it was heavy on the controls. It responded smartly to all my inputs, but the control stick felt like it was mounted in glue.

After a couple of takeoffs and landings, I relaxed on the stick for a moment to rest. The airplane continued to fly itself. I looked in the back seat and could see that Henry's hands and feet were still fast to the controls. He had been holding on all the time. He nodded and grinned a silent acknowledgement over the din of the engine, but never released his grip.

We flew to a small lake with high shorelines to explore the mysteries of glassy water landings. It was difficult to judge our height above the mirror-smooth surface. I set up a slow, nose-up approach, as shown in my book, but the lake was too small and I had to overshoot. Henry showed me how to use the shoreline for a height reference to descend into the lake in time. His landing was so smooth that the spray off the floats was the first indication that we had touched down.

For rough water practise, we used the middle of a large bay not far from town. Henry showed me a slow, full-flap approach for the landing. I thought the airplane was going to fall out of the sky. I knew the Cub would fly slowly, but our speed over the water was nearly zero on touchdown. We used full flap for the rough water takeoff. It was literally a hop, skip and a jump. The large motor easily hauled us into the air off the third wave.

In calmer water, Henry had me take off with the power reduced to 1700 RPM. This simulated a loaded departure on a hot day and gave me more time to follow the airplane through its take-off sequence. While taxiing back for another try (the only time we could talk), Henry asked me about the air regulations regarding night landings on floats.

"It's strictly forbidden," I replied.

"That's right, young fella. Landing here in the dark is like trying to floss a grizzly's teeth in the forest at midnight. That's why I'm going to show you how to do it now, in daylight. If you get caught out after dark, you might have a chance. First, plan to land on the other side of the point and taxi around with your lights off, because that's Bannister's house up there on the hill."

The rest of the night technique was basically a glassy water setup. Slowly descend below the limits of useful reference and hope you don't hit some poor sucker in an unlit canoe. I never did get caught out after dark, so I never suffered through the black hell of a night landing.

Henry crammed a great deal of training into the minimum required two hours, but as soon as the time was up, he motioned for me to head to the dock. I cut the power too far back and our momentum died short of the slip.

"Shall I paddle in the rest of the way?" I asked, thinking of the book.

"If you're hankering for exercise. If it was me, I would restart the engine and then I wouldn't miss my dinner."

I still needed three hours' practise on my own to complete the requirements for the float endorsement. Henry sent me solo that same day after some parting words of wisdom. "Remember, before soaring with the geese, you have to be a little chicken. Take it easy and fly yellow side up."

I flew the time off in two flights, finishing just before dark. It was fun. A great sense of freedom came with strapping into the Supercub, knowing that thousands of lakes and rivers beckoned with their endlessly varying conditions. I was hooked.

The solo time gave me a chance to relax and practise at my own pace. I revisited the different spots that I had flown into with Henry and repeated the take-off and landing techniques, but not the mistakes. When the time was up, the sun was low and I was bone tired from a long day, but I was happy. The next day I would start my career as a bush pilot, flying my first fire patrol.

While I was tying up the airplane, Henry ambled out of the office toward the dock. I called out to him, "Watch your step, that dock's slicker than snot on a doorknob."

His grin widened. "Say, you're catching on better than the measles. Now if we can get you out of those shiny shoes, we might make you into a bush pilot."

5/ HIGHER! HIGHER!

A body appeared on the dock beside the Supercub. It stood huddled in a ski jacket with its head bowed and shoulders raised so it seemed to have no neck. The eyes in the puffy face were closed.

I knew the body must belong to the observer from the Department of Soil and Sea because there was a portable radio transmitter lying at its feet, in the water washing over the dock.

I jumped down from the strut where I was checking the gas and introduced myself. "Hi, I'm your pilot for the fire patrol."

No reply.

"Well, it looks like we have a nice day. I've done the pre-flight and I'm ready to go whenever you are."

Still no response.

I moved closer for a better look.

A small slit sprang open in the swollen face to reveal one red eye. A few hoarse words were forced through the closed lips.

"Don't touch me." The voice sounded like it was full of broken glass.

This was my introduction to Gilbert Rooney, the junior ranger assigned to the fire patrol. He was there in body but not in soul. Gilbert had joined the Soil and Sea summer program because he loved wildlife; the type of wildlife a university student encounters far from home at a co-ed junior ranger camp. Gilbert was a party lover, and despite the strict ranger regulations against alcohol, he always managed to tie one on. The night before we met had been no exception.

I didn't know Gilbert's reputation, but I did recognize an acute hangover. Gilbert was suffering. The look on his sorry face told the story.

I wasn't going to let his condition dampen my enthusiasm. This was my first working flight in the bush. The Airways' contract called for taking a Department observer on at least two fire patrols a day if it wasn't raining. I had an observer, so I was going to do a fire patrol. I hoisted Gilbert's portable radio into the Cub's baggage compartment and began untying the lines. He obediently followed my

22

lead and slowly folded himself into the back seat.

I didn't know it at the time, but Gilbert hated flying as much as he loved partying. He had taken the observer's job only to avoid the real work assigned to the other rangers: hand planting trees in the logged-out regions of the bush. He had been counting on the spring rains to wash out most of the flights, but it had been unusually dry. Gilbert had already done a month of almost daily sorties, and there was no relief in sight. It was going to be a long summer.

Gilbert also knew that my presence on the dock that early morning meant that he was sentenced to fly with another rookie pilot. The thought of an extra-rough ride, wandering courses, and my ignorance of what fire patrolling was all about had left him speechless. He really didn't want to be there, but there was nothing he could do about it.

I taxied out for takeoff and turned to see if his seat belt was fastened. It was, but he hadn't rigged his radio or donned his headphones. One red eye peered through a slit and dared me to say something. I didn't. I shoved the throttle full forward and let the engine noise of the old bush plane speak for me.

Henry had given me a map of the patrol so I knew our rectangular route. Departing from the foot of Paradise, we flew southeasterly along the shore of Georgian Bay. The area was unique with its 30,000 rock islands hugging this edge of Lake Huron. There were hundreds of inlets, and it was hard to tell where the islands ended and the main shoreline began.

I flew reasonably straight and didn't get lost. Out of kindness to Gilbert, I climbed above the required one-thousand foot altitude to where the air was smoother. Marked on my map were mandatory observer call-in points designed to keep the smoke spotter awake. I turned to see if Gilbert was still there when we approached the first one. He was wearing his headphones, but he was slumped in the seat with his head back and his mouth open, sound asleep. We were plugged into different radios and we did not have an intercom. I tapped Gilbert's leg; the eyelids flickered; I motioned with my microphone. He raised his mike to his mouth and moved his lips briefly. His head fell back almost immediately.

At Happy Harbour we turned inland before reversing our course to fly northwesterly for an hour. This leg covered the Muskoka area with its jigsaw pattern of lakes and streams. I repeated the leg-tapping, microphone-waving routine at every checkpoint. Gilbert responded each time by mumbling into his mike and passing out again.

Reaching the Magnetic River, we followed it downstream toward Georgian Bay and turned for home. I didn't see any smoke. Neither did Gilbert.

The flight was a perfect way to gain experience. I was learning about the airplane and the area without the normal bush flying pressures of gauging loads, dealing with anxious passengers, flying in bad weather or landing at unfamiliar lakes. All that would come soon enough.

The end of the patrol brought the welcome chance to stretch my legs and slap some circulation into my backside. Gilbert's nightmare wasn't over. We were scheduled to take a break while the aircraft was being refueled and then we had to squeeze into it again for another two hours and thirty-five minutes.

Today, forest fire detection is flown in high-speed twin-engine aircraft capable of covering our patrol area in twenty minutes, and soon may be taken over by the two-minute pass of a satellite. But at that time a Piper Supercub on floats was considered the best means of fire patrolling.

The refueling was done by Sam Pettigrew, the Airways' dockhand. Sam was the manager's son. He was a pleasant, simple kid, born with a permanent grin. Sam normally moved with the slowness of someone who, at only sixteen, had gone as far as he was going to get in life.

Unfortunately for Gilbert, Sam attached great urgency to putting the fire patrol back into the air. When we taxied up to the dock, he ceased to be a one-speed man and quickly started gassing the airplane while I was still tying up.

Gilbert was awake and moving around. He still looked like an old corpse, but his sleep must have healed some of the damage. He climbed out of the Cub and yelled up to Sam, "I hate you Sam Pettigrew!"

Sam was obviously familiar with Gilbert, because he kept on smiling and didn't stop fueling. Gilbert placed an orange crate across the gas hose on the dock and sat on it. It probably didn't impede the flow in the big hose, but it made him feel better. When I sat next to him, he apologized for his unfriendly behavior and thanked me for waking him up at the check points.

"Don't mention it," I replied. "I was glad to help. Besides, that was your flight. The next one is mine, and I'm going to fly it inverted so you can watch for smoke with your head tilted back."

He flashed a nervous smile, unsure that I was kidding.

Not long into our second patrol, I found a smoke. A thin column of it drifted up from the bush beside a long, narrow bay in Go Home Lake. I found the smoke because Gilbert was sleeping again. When I woke him up, he automatically started calling in the next checkpoint. I gestured madly at the ground. Gilbert motioned for me to circle.

When I flew over the spot, neither one of us could see the origin of the fire because the smoke filtered up through a thick canopy of trees. Cottages dotted the water's edge, but no burning permits had been issued for that area. If we could determine that this blaze was unattended, then Gilbert would call for a crew to come and douse it. If the smoke was just from a cottager burning brush illegally, then headquarters would dispatch an officer with a warning or fine.

Since our communication was limited, I gestured to Gilbert that I was going to fly low over the water so he could look in under the covering forest and hopefully see the fire. He nodded as if he understood.

I saw four strands of hydro wires stretched across the bay near the smoke. They hung about ten metres above the water, but I estimated if we skimmed over the surface we would be able to pass under them with plenty of room to spare. I reduced the power on the Supercub, descended toward the opening of the bay and levelled off with the floats almost touching the water. I concentrated on the wires ahead, knowing Gilbert would check out the fire. Over the roar of the engine I could hear him yell, "Higher!"

I figured that he couldn't see over the shoreline, so I eased the control stick back and milked the airplane up a bit, still leaving clearance below the wires.

Gilbert shouted even louder, "Higher!"

We were nearly at the hydro lines, but I thought I could give him half our remaining clearance so I nudged the airplane up farther. It looked awfully close as we flashed underneath.

I added full power and pulled up before we reached the end of the bay. I turned in my seat to check Gilbert's verdict on the fire; he wasn't there. He was on the floor. Normally that would have been impossible, but Gilbert had been trying to warn me of the hydro lines. He had been shouting "Wires", not "Higher", and with every warning, I had climbed closer to the menacing strands. He was certain that we were going to hit, so he had compressed himself into a terrified mass on the tiny floor. The biggest parts of his body were his red eyes.

He hadn't seen the fire. He started screaming when I indicated another pass. I tried to tell him that I saw the wires, but he stayed on the floor. Flying on the water again, I looked left as we passed under the hydro lines. A cottager happily waved at us from his dock.

I helped Gilbert up from where he was wedged between our seats. He was awake.

6/ NEVER HAVE TO SAY YOU'RE SORRY

The weather stayed hot and dry, and I flew double fire patrols every day. By the end of my first week, I was well vibrated, but happy. I felt like I had made it. I was now a bona fide bush pilot and to prove it I had ringing ears and a tan from the neck up.

Until I met Dexter Sweeney, I had been hoping that the good flying weather would last forever. Dexter was my first revenue passenger after Gilbert Rooney. As he and I circled over a rocky island campsite in the Supercub, I was thinking that I would rather be anywhere else. Below were three men looking up from their fish cleaning chores. Dexter pointed down, indicating that I should land beside them.

The island was in the Pickerel River. The area was unique with its ancient rock stripped of soil and worn smooth by a long-departed glacier. The run-off in this region formed an exceptionally clear stream and was favored by pickerel and trout.

This was a wide section of the river, and I had no problem landing between shoals. I shut down and opened the airplane's door as we coasted toward the shore. The three men stood by the edge, waiting for a clue to our visit. Dexter was first to speak, calling from the back seat of the drifting Cub.

"How's the fishing, boys?" he said with his face set in a cat-that-got-the-canary smile.

"Fine," one of them replied. All three wore puzzled expressions. They had no reason to recognize either Dexter or myself.

Dexter continued his friendly manner, "Let's see your catch."

The men were happy to oblige. One of them bent over and pulled a chain from the water that contained a string of at least thirty shining fish. It was Dexter's cue. He donned the peaked cap that he had hidden in the baggage compartment and climbed out onto the airplane's float as we neared the shore.

"My name is Dexter Sweeney and by the power vested in me by the Department of Soil and Sea, I am searching this camp for further evidence of actions that contravene the fish and game laws."

Sweeney's smile was gone and his voice had changed to a poor

26

imitation of Humphrey Bogart. He jumped to shore as the Cub nudged the rocks. The fishermen's puzzled expressions turned to concern as they grasped what was happening.

What was happening was Dexter Sweeney, champion of justice and saviour of dead fish. Dexter was the local game warden and his self-styled purpose in life was to ruin tourists' holidays. Warden Sweeney puffed up his scrawny frame and continued, "I expect no trouble from you gentlemen, but please stay where you are while I look around."

Dexter Sweeney worked for the Department of Soil and Sea District Office across the harbour from the Airways' docks in Paradise. The base didn't have its own aircraft, so a good percentage of our business came from transporting its staff. Our least favorite was the game warden.

Sweeney possessed the narrow, beady eyes and slimy sneer of someone that you would like to bop on the nose for just looking at you. Henry described him as, "sour as a polecat caught in a trap." Dexter attacked his job with a zeal out of proportion to its importance. He loved it. He assumed everyone in the world was guilty of poaching and he was out to catch them all.

He wouldn't make a flight booking in advance, because he believed the Airways staff would spread word of his activities, spoiling his effectiveness. Instead, he would call up and speak in the hushed tones of a Hollywood spy and ask Beverly if there was an aircraft available immediately.

If one of the pilots was in the office, he would give her a big head-shaking, arm-waving "NO." Besides not liking the guy or his methods, the flying staff harboured a genuine fear of being shot. A tourist with too many fish was no problem, but we all dreaded the day Sweeney might catch a professional poacher deep in the bush. He always carried a .38 calibre revolver, but it would be no contest against locals carrying high-powered rifles who might find no witnesses preferable to jail.

If Pettigrew was in when he called, Gary would gladly make the arrangements. He didn't have to fly with Sweeney, and it was his job to make the Airways profitable. He had booked me with the game warden for this trip.

Sweeney had arrived in his unmarked car and approached our office in a silly commando crouch. He spotted me standing beside the flight sheets and barked through the screen door, "Come on, let's go."

Henry had warned me to stand my ground with this guy. The weather was good, but in case of mechanical trouble, I was required to tell Beverly where we were headed.

"Where are we going?" I asked.

"I can't divulge that information until we are airborne or she'll

27

tell everyone," he replied, pointing an accusing finger at Beverly.

He was a comical character to watch, and I was having difficulty being intimidated by him, despite his best efforts. "Maybe you should handcuff her away from the phone," I teased. "I need to know our direction."

He eyed me, trying to measure my resolve, and muttered, "North, maybe."

Henry had told me what to say. "Beverly, we are flying north along the shore of Georgian Bay, not further than the Pickerel River."

We taxied out, and Sweeney ordered me to fly south first and then swing north over open water, once we were out of sight of town.

"I must take off northbound to be into the wind," I explained truthfully, but after lifting off, I flew low up Main Street. It did nothing to warn poachers, but I enjoyed aggravating the man.

The object of those flights was to locate fishermen in remote areas, land beside them and check their catches. This let the sportsmen in the area know that they were being monitored, hopefully discouraging the greedy ones from stripping the lakes of fish. But Sweeney's attitude was never to use a flyswatter when a sledgehammer would do. If he found tourists with one fish over their allowable limits, he would chew them out, confiscate their equipment and catch, and issue fines. He accomplished the objective of preserving wildlife by discouraging visitors from ever returning to the region.

By the time we had reached the Pickerel River on this day's patrol, we had stopped twice and observed overcatches both times. The Cub's tiny baggage compartment was crammed with smelly fish and tangled poles. Sweeney was as restless as a shark on the scent of blood. The men on this island were just what he wanted.

I sat on a rock and held a line to the airplane, trying to look detached from the scene. The three sportsmen watched the relentless warden strut around their campsite. He pulled two other heavy strings of fish from the river, which meant these guys had exceeded the bounds of just "a few extra fish." Sweeney was in his raving glory.

"My pilot has already informed me that we have no more room for confiscated goods so I order you men to release the fish on those strings. Since you are seriously over your limits, you won't be needing these anymore." He picked up some very expensive-looking fishing rods and tossed them into the river.

The oldest of the men started to protest, but that just launched Sweeney into a lecture about how he had the power to confiscate everything at the campsite, because of the size of their overcatch. He threw their remaining fishing gear into the river. I'm sure he would have taken their motorboat if he could have figured a way to fly it behind the Supercub.

The three men bent to the task of releasing the fish. Fortunately for all of us, they didn't seem to be the kind to make any serious trouble. They had been caught breaking the law and they seemed to accept their fate, but Sweeney's attitude was so hostile he could have enraged a fairy godmother.

The tensions on the island came to a head when the little ferret burst out of the campers' tent carrying a large rifle with a scope. He stood on his tiptoes and screeched, "And what was this for, shooting fish?"

"We brought it for some target practice," one of them answered lamely.

"There is no game in season that warrants carrying this kind of weapon. Under the law, I can only assume you are hunting illegally."

He held the gun barrel like a baseball bat and gave it a homerun swing, sending it upstream with the rest of their gear. One of the men actually made a move toward him as the gun went sailing. I crouched behind a rock. Sweeney reacted by turning to face the man in a ridiculous John Wayne stance, his right hand hovering over the holstered .38. The guy stopped moving.

Sweeney seemed satisfied that he had made his point and done all the damage he could. He pulled out his violation book and took their names. The older man was James Boyd. The name didn't mean anything to me, but it had a paralyzing effect on Sweeney. Apparently Boyd had been a radio personality in his younger days. He had been the radio voice of Sweeney's favourite boyhood hero.

Sweeney looked up from the man's fishing licence and said in a low voice, "You're Ranger Ron."

"That's right. Did you listen to my show?"

"Listen; yes, I heard you every Thursday. I'm Dexter Sweeney; I was an official Ranger Ron Little Ranger. I wrote you a letter, and you sent me a badge and an autographed picture of you on your horse."

Sweeney looked stricken. He realized what he had just done to his big hero. Boyd stood there, not knowing what to do.

"Gee Ranger Ron, I mean Mr. Boyd, I'm sorry that I threw all your gear into the river."

There was an awkward silence until Boyd finally smiled and said, "You know that rule number four in the Little Ranger Code of the West was, 'Never have to say you're sorry.'" The remark drained some of the tension from the air.

Sweeney smiled ruefully and replied, "I suppose if the show was still on, you would have to announce my name as a bad Little Ranger."

The radio cowboy said, "Well, I guess you're only doing your job."

A changed Sweeney closed his violation book and said, "Look, the fish are back where they belong and your tackle is gone, so let's call it even." Extending his hand, he added, "I'm sorry we didn't meet under better circumstances, Mr. Boyd. I'll be going now."

The big man accepted the handshake, "I guess now it's my turn to say I'm sorry. Good-bye."

Sweeney headed toward me, shooing me into the airplane. I fired up and took off for home. All the way back, he stared off into the distance.

When I was helping him unload the Cub, he stopped for a moment and fixed me with his official game warden look. "See to it that no one else knows what happened out there today," he ordered.

"Yes sir, Mr. Sweeney."

"Good."

That night I joined the other Airways pilots for a beer at the Queen's Hotel. Oscar Fleming, the lineman for Bannister Cable TV, came in wearing a grin, "I hear you were up flying with your friend Dexter."

He was trying to get a rise out of me, but I wasn't paying much attention to him. I had spotted three familiar fishermen in the corner and I was wondering what Dexter might think if he knew that Ranger Ron poached fish AND drank beer.

7/ STONEFACE

Except for the flight with Sweeney, it felt good to get away from flying with student pilots. I hadn't realized how much energy was required to control an airplane using someone else's inexperienced brain and untrained limbs. Patrolling some of the country's best scenery with Gilbert asleep in the back was relaxing in comparison.

I was beginning to forget that teaching was part of my job description, but Pettigrew hadn't. He was anxious for me to upgrade my instructor's rating so he could line up students. He booked me a Department of Transport flight test for the next week.

I had already written the exam and I met the hourly requirements for the next level rating. I just needed to demonstrate on the flight test that I had become an above average flying instructor and then I could teach on my own. I was rapidly getting comfortable with the airplane and I felt confident about the test.

The instructor standards inspector agreed to meet me at the floatplane dock beside the Toronto Island Airport. On the appointed day, I took the other Cub because it had a working compass. As I climbed out from Paradise, it was so clear that it looked like I should be able to see Toronto, two hundred kilometres to the south. The morning warmth promised a hot day for early May.

At Barrie, about halfway, the forward visibility began to drop because of haze, the curse of flying toward an industrialized area. As I approached Toronto, the horizon disappeared and I could see only five kilometres ahead. To reach the city's harbour, I needed to penetrate a net of three airport control zones spread left to right across the middle of town: Buttonville, the Downsview military base, and Toronto International. The alternative was detouring around them all and being late for my test. Since Buttonville was a general aviation airport, I flew a compass heading in that direction.

Many pilots flying VFR (Visual Flight Rules) would not have flown in that thick haze. The ones who would, hoped that everyone else had decided not to. See-and-be-seen separation was impossible. I tuned in Buttonville Tower and listened ahead. The controller was busy. He was using a staccato delivery to keep everyone apart in the smog. I waited until I knew I must be entering his zone and then broke in to the frequency.

"Buttonville Tower, this is Lima Alpha India, a Supercub on floats from Paradise entering your zone."

"LAI, standby; break, TIQ you are number five to the One-Fifty, keep him in sight and call base; ZEF call overhead; PPT keep the power up, I'll get you away after this next one."

I flew on, listening to the acknowledgements from the other aircraft. The farmland below had disappeared abruptly, and I was over endless squares of streets and houses.

"LAI, are you going to the Island?"

"Affirmative, LAI," I replied.

"Call overhead, LAI; advise any altitude change; altimeter 30.23."

"LAI."

Since I wasn't exactly sure where I was, the little mistake of not giving my destination made me feel stupid. I continued on, leaning forward to see through the haze. The talk on the radio indicated that the sky must have been filled with airplanes, but I didn't see any. I didn't recognize any landmarks below until I crossed an enormous road about twelve lanes wide. It was Highway 401 running east/west through Toronto. I had flown right through Buttonville's control zone and out the other side. I continued to fly south, hoping the controller would forget about me.

"LAI, are you overhead yet?"

"Actually sir, I'm crossing the 401." My sudden honesty made me feel better.

"What does your compass say, LAI?"

"One-hundred and eighty degrees, sir."

"Good, that means you are leaving us, you're cleared enroute; break, RZL, cleared to land, keep the speed up, I've got four behind you and six to go."

I was lucky that he was too busy to say more. I had screwed up, and his tone said that he wanted me to know that he knew.

I followed the Don Valley Parkway southbound. It was jammed with cars and lined with apartment buildings. I felt naked flying over it on floats. An engine failure on wheels would have been just as disasterous, but somehow the idea seemed worse on pontoons. I tuned in Toronto Island Tower when I reached Lake Ontario. They were busy too.

"Island Tower, Lima Alpha India, a Supercub on floats from Paradise, entering your zone at Don Valley for landing in the harbour."

"LAI, call by the stack for landing westbound; wind 240 at 10, altimeter 30.22."

"LAI."

Great; the waterfront was covered with stacks, and I didn't know which one was supposed to be "the stack." I headed for the biggest one.

Toronto's natural harbour was formed by a series of interconnected islands curving out into Lake Ontario. The protected water was about three kilometres long and two wide.

"LAI is by the stack."

"LAI, roger; land in the harbour at your discretion; watch for debris."

I had heard the precaution about debris before and I always thought it referred to the logs and Javex bottles common to harbours. Lined up for a landing in a floatplane, I saw that he meant boats. I was looking at a maze of ferrys, sailboats, tugs, and motorboats. They were all darting madly about like ants at a picnic.

I throttled back, extended the flaps and descended purposefully toward the water. It didn't intimidate anyone. There was no space to land. I started an overshoot and called the tower.

"Call by the stack," he replied.

It wasn't any better the second time. I felt like an old lady trying to cross a busy street against the light. The controller wasn't too happy about another overshoot, because it conflicted with his runway traffic.

"Call by the stack, LAI. I promise you the harbour will be clear if you come back at Christmas."

I noticed the large ferrys were leaving a brief open path in their wake, so I turned in behind one and descended. I touched down in the calm by the stern, but my speed carried me across his wake. The waves didn't look significant from above, but as I skated towards them, they grew. I hit them with enough speed to bounce me back into the air. The splash that followed was spectacular, but nothing fell off and the airplane was still floating. I taxied up to the floatplane dock and shut down.

The inspector was waiting for me. I knew it was the inspector, because he was the only one on the dock dressed like an undertaker. He was an older man with a very stern look on his face. He must have witnessed my arrival.

"I'm Inspector Kennedy from the Department of Transport. Are you the Class II candidate from Paradise?" he said without smiling.

"Yes sir. I'm pleased to meet you," I replied with a big grin and an outstretched hand.

He accepted the handshake, giving me one terse pump, but he didn't return the smile.

"I wasn't sure you were the one. Most candidates at this level don't arrive in jeans, sneakers and no tie." This man was not full of joy. "Did you bring your licence, maps and flight planning equipment?"

"Yes sir."

"Let's go into the flying school for the ground portion of the test," he said.

When we were seated at a table, he checked my licence and said, "Fifty percent of the candidates on this flight test fail to upgrade."

"Oh?" was all I could think of in reply. I wondered what had happened to the government testing manual that said the candidate is to be greeted in a friendly manner.

He asked me to demonstrate a cross-country planning lesson to the Keene Waterdrome on Rice Lake, an hour northeast of Toronto. I spent the rest of the morning doing that and I thought it went well, although I couldn't tell by looking at his face. During the whole briefing, he sat stonelike, saying little and smiling not at all.

Next I was to demonstrate the cross-country in the air as if it was his first navigation lesson. As the instructor, I would be flying the airplane from the back seat. I had never done that before. Inspector Kennedy said that he would do the radio work for me.

I pushed off from the dock and climbed into the back. He was a big man, and I could see nothing forward except his shoulders. I dug out a life jacket from the baggage compartment and sat on it. With my head jammed against the tubing in the roof, I could see past either side of his head. The view was filled with boats.

"Would you like to do the takeoff sir?" I asked hopefully.

"No. Tell me when you are ready, and I'll call the tower."

I circled around while pretending to check the magnetos and the controls. I finally saw an opening behind a ferry. I told Kennedy that I was ready. I accelerated in the short open space behind the big boat and with full flap, we had enough lift to use the wake to catapult us into the air.

I headed northeast and settled down for some serious navigation. The visibility was still just five kilometres in haze. It was hard work. There was no horizon to fix a heading so I was continually wandering back and forth. I shouted heading corrections and ground speed checks into Kennedy's ear that were mostly a guess. I could map read straight down until we entered the nothingness past Oshawa. Then I was lost. I just hoped that Kennedy didn't realize that I didn't know where we were until we flew over something I could recognize.

He knew. He turned in his seat and yelled, "Where are we?"

I looked outside once more and got the lucky break of a lifetime. In the absolute middle of nowhere, we were flying over Mosport. As an avid car racing fan, I instantly recognized the twisting pavement of the famous race course. It was marked on my map, so I triumphantly showed Kennedy.

Next, he had me demonstrate slow flight, stalls and steep turns. I think the haze saved me during these manoeuvres. With the inspector blocking my view, I had little reference for altitude, heading and airspeed control, but with the milky haze, he had just as little to go by to judge my performance.

During these exercises, I worked the airplane north, looking for better weather. When I completed a forced approach demonstration, Kennedy told me to show him a low-level cross-country diversion back to Toronto Island. Our course took us through Buttonville's control zone. I asked him to call for a clearance.

I could just make out the radio communications over the cabin speaker. It was the same controller. He was still busy, but Kennedy expertly butted in, "Buttonville Tower, this is Lima Alpha India, a Supercub on floats, northeast, requesting clearance through your zone to Toronto Island."

"LAI, Buttonville, I want you to stay out of my control zone, unless you are absolutely sure of your position."

I could see the red shoot up the back of Kennedy's neck in response to the controller's unusual request.

"I am exactly over Stouffville now," he replied in a stern voice.

"Congratulations LAI, call overhead the airport and let me know if you get lost."

His neck was now beet red and the little hairs were sticking straight out. These transmissions were sandwiched in between the many calls to and from other aircraft. Kennedy had a powerful sense of radio discipline because all he said in reply was, "LAI."

I did my part, map reading to beat the band. I made sure that we flew right over the middle of the airport in the haze.

"LAI is overhead," Kennedy said.

"Very good LAI, now see if you can find your way southbound and call crossing the 401."

"LAI."

When we got back to the harbour, I willed a good landing on the first pass. I knew Kennedy must have been preoccupied with the dressing down he had received at Buttonville and I didn't want to do anything that would make him think it was my fault. I used a ferry for a blocker again, sideslipping with full flap to land far enough behind it to stay out of its wake.

Back in the Island's flying school office, Kennedy told me that I had passed. "You had better be on your way," he said. "I'm going to call Buttonville Tower and find out what that was all about before they change shifts."

He didn't offer me a handshake or a smile and I didn't care. I just wanted out of there with my new rating. I knew he might be looking for me when the controller explained the origin of LAI's less-than-stirling reputation. I took off immediately and hoped that I would never see the man again.

8/ FALLING HERO

I expected to find a stern message waiting from Inspector Kennedy when I landed at Paradise. There was none. I was now qualified to teach on my own, but the next day I was back fire patrolling. By the end of my second week I still didn't have any customers for flying lessons. Pettigrew had given me some leads, but after five hours in the Supercub each day, I couldn't make myself call them. Perhaps I was spending too much time with work-shy Gilbert Rooney and enjoying it.

Gary took the matter into his own hands and soon announced that he had drummed up my first student customer. Actually, the man had walked into the office looking for lessons, but Pettigrew took the credit anyway. When I met the new student, Pettigrew was dancing around with dollar signs in his eyes, trying to indicate that this was someone important. He didn't have to; I recognized the man right away. He was Ian Westley, one of my real live personal heroes.

As a fan of auto racing, I read everything I could about the international events. Ian Westley was one of the few Canadians who raced in the highest level of the sport. He never won and often finished last. Ian was a second-string driver on a third-rate team, but that didn't matter to me; he was a Canadian driver my own age who had raced in the big leagues and that was enough to qualify him for hero status. In real life, Ian looked the part. He was dressed casually and stood confidently. He gave me a firm handshake and a warm smile.

After two years in the top circuit, Ian had decided there must be more to life than trying to be second-last in an uncompetitive car. He hung up his Nomex in favor of relaxing at his parent's cottage for the summer and learning to fly. Pettigrew was excited, not by his good looks, but by the fact that the man was exceedingly rich.

We arranged that I would fly a Supercub out to the Westley's island cottage for Ian's daily lessons. Ian was a quick study. He was well co-ordinated, enthusiastic, and easy to teach. He was learning to fly faster than I had, but it was impossible to dislike him. Besides being smart and rich, Ian was charming and interesting to be around.

Up to that time, my new life as a bush pilot had been a very narrow triangle; I flew the fire patrol, ate at the Kentucky Fried Chicken outlet and, through Pettigrew's doubtful generosity, slept on the sofa in the pilot's shack. The flying was fun, the chicken I could live with, but the accommodation was disgusting. The linoleum floor in the shack was curled and cracked like old parchment and thick layers of dingy paint were chipped and peeling. The smell of stale cigarettes, old beer and fried chicken clung to everything. I couldn't afford a motel, so it had to do until I found a permanent place to stay.

Meeting Ian changed things considerably. The two of us sat on his dock sipping lemonade served by a pretty maid during our preflight briefings. Ian was easily sidetracked into telling racing stories. While Pettigrew sat back in his office imagining that I was flying the floats off the Supercub, I would be reclining on the Westley's dock hanging onto Ian's description of the Canadian Grand Prix at the Mont Tremblant Racetrack, where he unsuccessfully took a chicane flat out.

Near mealtimes, Mrs. Westley always insisted that I join the family. Normal fare was smoked salmon pate, Caesar salad, beef chateaubriande and black forest cake served on gilded china, with white linen and ornate silver. The Westleys thought this was cottage living, because they did not have a string quartet playing dinner music in the background. It was a treat to rub elbows with these kind people, but a little embarrassing for me. Ian was built like a jockey, and the whole family ate like birds. It was difficult not to draw attention to myself, as I inhaled all that great food. When we were done each lesson, I would fly back to my other life and try to explain to Gary why it took me four hours to get one hour's revenue.

On Ian's fourth lesson, we returned to Paradise where there was more open water to practise takeoffs and landings. We didn't use the flaps because the pin holding the flap lever in its extended position was worn and occasionally would let go. If this happened, the flaps would self-retract, spilling lift from the wings, and the airplane would drop like a wounded duck. Negative "g" forces would cause years of lost pencils, coins and fish hooks to float up in front of the pilot's face. With added power, the plane recovered quickly, and the debris would rain down to find its way back into the hiding places in the floor.

The slipping pin was potentially dangerous, but we all knew about it, and since the Supercub had bags of extra performance, we could land and take off most of the time without using flaps. If we were working into a particularly tight spot, then we held the flap lever with one hand and flew with the other.

The Westley's cottage was located in a tight spot. It was on a winding narrow inlet complete with wires, channel markers and boat traffic. In the rear seat of the Supercub, I had a duplicate control stick, rudder pedals and throttle, but Ian had the only flap lever. I briefed him before the flight on how to handle the final approach at his cottage, remembering the faulty pin.

Ian reduced power for the landing, pushed forward on the stick to set up a glide and moved his left hand to extend and hold the flaps. This made the airplane pitch up and lose speed. Instead of pushing the nose down into a steeper approach, Ian let go of the flap lever to apply power. The faulty pin released and the sudden loss of lift forced the Cub into a rapid sink. It felt like we were going down a children's slide on a piece of waxed paper. This was too much for Ian: he released everything, covered his eyes and screamed.

It was far from a dangerous situation, but to a novice, macho race driver or not, it looked like the end. He thought we were going in. To recover, I shoved forward on my stick, momentarily floating us in our harnesses. Regaining speed, I easily flared out over the surface and touched down with a gentle splash in front of the dock. He took away his hands and stared in disbelief. His face was bleached white with a greenish tinge, and he was shaking. I mentally kicked myself for letting the situation go too far. Because of his racing experience, I had assumed Ian would react more competently than other novice students faced with the same problem.

My next job was to smooth over what had happened, so he didn't go sour on flying lessons. I didn't do very well. With a vivid image of Ian screaming his head off as we gently touched the surface, I had to bite my lip to hold a concerned look. I explained how he would be able to handle similar situations by the end of this thirty-lesson course, but he saw through my mask. Anger and humiliation flushed his face and the race car driver in him took over.

"Never mind the end of the course, we are going back up now."

Over the wires, between the markers and boats, we practised repeated approaches. When the flap lever didn't self-retract, Ian would release it on purpose. It was getting dark, and we were nearly out of gas when he finally felt that he could consistently cope with the situation.

When I let him off at the dock he said, "I feel better now, but we won't be even until I see you in a race car approaching Mosport's Esses at speed with a stuck throttle."

9/ WELCOME TO PARADISE

I didn't have much time to look for a place to live for Susan and me. Every day brought good weather, keeping me busy with fire patrols and flying lessons. The lumpy couch reminded me that time was running out, when I came back every night to the pilot's shack.

I did look whenever I could, unsuccessfully. When I met a new face, I asked about accommodation; no luck there either. It was a problem. There were numerous places to stay, but the key word was affordable. Paradise was a vacation centre with plenty of housing – for tourists. Motels, resorts, boarding houses, cabins and campsites were all gearing up for another season. The prices were set to make their owners a year's income over the next four months. I found that we could rent a tiny cottage in the woods by a lake for three times my salary.

The rest of the town was a small community with no apartment buildings. When a couple married, they either built a house or lived with their parents until a relative died and left them a place. It was depressing.

When I told Susan, she suggested coming and helping me on the weekend. I agreed. She ought to see Paradise before she moved in. Susan was the kind of person who made up her mind and stuck to it. If she liked the town, the accommodation wouldn't be too critical. If she didn't . . . ; well, we would deal with that when it happened.

Pettigrew gave me Saturday afternoon off after the fire patrols so I could meet Susan's bus. She wasn't really a bus person so she looked niggled when she got off. It didn't help that the stop for Paradise was outside town at a highway gas station.

The way she was dressed made her look out of place. She had on a plaid shirt, jeans and hiking boots, which sounds just perfect for up north, but on Susan they were a fashion statement. She was wearing full make-up and the beautifully pressed plaid shirt was outlined by the straps of a matching knapsack and topped with a contrasting jacket hung over her shoulders. The perfectly factory faded designer jeans were stuffed into the top of a pair of polished Kodiaks. Despite the long bus ride, she looked like she had stepped out of a safari fashion catalogue.

"Hi. Welcome to Paradise," I said. "There is more to it than this, believe me." We had been apart for two weeks and it was good to see her. I gave her a big kiss.

"It can't be a much of a place," she said, "The bus driver was surprised when I told him that this was where I wanted to get off."

"The actual town is up this side road. Come on, I'll show you around."

We drove down Main Street. The largest shop in town was Bannister's Family Discount Store. The windows featured the latest in pedal pushers, yellow rubber boots and sweatshirts depicting bears fishing in a stream over the caption, "Paradise — We're Glad You Came."

"Why is half the town painted that awful yellow and red?"

"Those are Mr. Bannister's favorite colors. I bet you could get a job in his store."

"I suppose; if I wanted to. But let's find a place to stay first."

We stopped at the real estate office. I had been there before, but it didn't hurt to check. Nothing. We bought a *Bannister Bugle*, the weekly paper. Nothing. Susan suggested that we try the laundromat bulletin board. Nothing. We drove around.

I showed her as many positive things about Paradise as I could find: the clear stream bubbling over rocks through the middle of town on its way to the harbour, the Moonbeam Drive-In Movie Theatre that was open every Friday night in the summer if it didn't rain, and Lookout Point that divided the water around Paradise into two bays.

"This seems like a nice town," she said casually. It was a good sign. "It's too bad there is nowhere to live," she added seriously.

I took her to the Airways and introduced her to everyone there. I hoped she would feel a part of the place. Gary Pettigrew was especially charming, in his meek little way.

After they had exchanged pleasantries, Susan said quite innocently, "Why can't we find a place to stay here?"

Her directness caught us both by surprise. Pettigrew sputtered, trying to come up with a reply. I wondered if she was going to get me fired.

When he caught his breath, Pettigrew said, "I'm sure something can be arranged. What did you have in mind?" He was talking to Susan, but he was looking at me. I decided since she had come this far, I wasn't going to interfere. I said nothing.

"We were hoping to rent a little cottage by the water, but the cost would have to reflect our income." Then she added as an inspiration, "Do you think that you and Mr. Bannister might be able to arrange something?"

The mention of Bannister made him wince, but he remained

charming. "Why don't you leave it with me and I'll see what I can do? In the meantime, perhaps we could talk your husband into taking you up in the Supercub for a short flight to show you the area, on the company of course."

I think the suggestion was made to get rid of us, before Susan came up with more ideas for him to work on with Bannister. He did emphasize that it be a short flight, but I appreciated his attempt to make her feel welcome.

"Thank you," Susan replied. "That would be nice."

Susan had flown with me many times before, but it was always on two days' notice and after taking several Gravol pills. I was keen to share my new-found love of float flying with her so I didn't suggest that we wait.

I signed out and led her down to the dock. She stopped short of the slightly submerged, slimy planks and looked at her shiny boots.

"Come on," I said, "You'll have to break in your garb sometime, but watch your step, the dock is slicker than snot on a doorknob."

"What a disgusting thing to say." she said. "I think you've been living here too long without me."

She tiptoed to the Supercub, and we went flying. The middle of the afternoon was the bumpiest time of day, so I kept the flight very short. The bushplane's heavy smell of dead fish and gasoline didn't help her stomach either, but Susan smiled gamely from the back seat without ever looking down.

After the flight, the two of us went to the pilot's shack and discussed our plans for the rest of the weekend. Sitting in the lumpy chairs amidst the old fried chicken wrappers, cigarette butts and empty beer bottles, Susan said, "Where do you sleep?"

"Here."

She wrinkled her nose.

"Where am I staying tonight?" she asked.

"Here?" I replied.

"I don't think so," she said.

I gave in to the suggestion that we splurge on a motel since we were newlyweds. Besides, the look on Susan's face told me that otherwise I might be sleeping alone. Neither one of us anticipated running headlong into the Paradise small-town mentality.

We went to the Stardust Motel on the highway. It was a ten-unit, plywood strip of rooms painted a fading baby blue. The heavy woman in the office nodded when we entered and gave us a long look up and down as we approached the desk.

"Good afternoon," I said, "We would like a single room for one night, please."

"With a double bed," Susan added with a smile.

The woman stared at us, working her gums together and flexing the warts on her cheeks, but she didn't say anything right away.

When she finally spoke, she said, "You two married?"

Susan turned scarlet. I said, "Yes."

"You got rings?" the woman asked.

"Yes," I replied.

"Let's see."

I would have just shown her, but Susan took over.

"Has this man come in here before with other girls?" she asked.

The question didn't seem to faze the woman.

"No, never seen him before in my life."

"That's good," she said, holding her ring finger practically up the woman's nose, "because he is my husband. I would appreciate it if you would let me know if he ever does come here with someone else. In the meantime, we would like a room."

The outburst seemed like something the woman could relate to. She pushed a registration card and a key across the desk. While I filled it in, she said, "Room Ten, at the end, in case you make too much noise."

Rather than being put off by the encounter, Susan thought it was a laugh. "Do you have any other funny old biddies like that in this town?" she asked with a giggle.

"I hope not," I replied.

Susan left the next day on the southbound bus—same driver. I promised to continue looking for accommodation without taking any other girls to the Stardust Motel.

10/ MULLIGAN STEWED

The notation on our booking sheets under Supercub read:

Pick up One—Mulligan's

no bags"18:00"G.

That translated into, "Fly the Supercub empty to Mulligan's cottage by 6 p.m., pick up one passenger, no luggage and return to Paradise". The "G" indicated that I was to be the pilot, but it had been originally booked with Jake, one of the other Airways pilots.

"Bev, how come I'm booked on Jake's charter at six o'clock?"

"Oh, Jake changed that. He said it was okay with Henry."

I was immediately suspicious. Jake Lewis was middle-aged with thinning, dark hair and a slight paunch. His most outstanding feature was his love for practical jokes.

Jake flew because it was more fun than driving a cab, which he did during the winter. Flying put beer on the table after work. Drinking the beer used up the flying money, so every day he went back to work. It was a vicious circle, but Jake's main purpose in life was to have fun.

Gary Pettigrew was Jake's main target for practical jokes because Gary gave him the best reaction, but I knew my turn would come. With this thought in mind, I asked Jake about the Mulligan charter later that day.

"Well," he said seriously, "I could see that my bookings were getting pretty tight today, so I asked Henry if you could do that one for me."

"And Henry said it was okay?" I asked.

"Sure. Let me show you where it is."

Henry's wall map indicated that Mulligan's cottage was on an outer island along the shore of Georgian Bay only twenty minutes away. I had already flown two fire patrols that day, but I welcomed the variety of a passenger flight. Charters were what real bush flying was all about.

To convince me, Jake added, "Mulligan is a real nice guy. I took him in last week. He doesn't say much, but he smiles a lot and tips big."

When I flew over Mulligan's island, I could see it was a long, narrow slash of rock and small trees, standing guard on the edge of the open bay. It was neatly arranged crossways to the prevailing wind, providing a calm surface along its lee side. The Supercub was not built to withstand a landing in the heavy swells usually found in open waters. I touched down close to the protecting shore.

A short man shaped like a bowling pin emerged from the cottage as I taxied toward the dock. He walked funny. He tottered like an infant, holding his arms in the air away from his large belly. He swayed from side to side with each step.

His funny wobble gained momentum on the slope to the water's edge. As his speed increased, his stubby legs had trouble keeping up with his body. By the time he reached the flats before the shore, he was tottering pell-mell, but his face was split by a wide grin. I shut down the engine to coast to the dock.

Still on his feet, the one-man welcoming party stumbled the length of the dock toward me. When I was still ten metres away, he waddled right off the end into the bay, still wearing his silly grin. He went straight to the bottom and didn't come up.

For a moment I stared at the receding splash in disbelief. As the Supercub drifted over the spot, I swung down onto the airplane's float. I could see his outline struggling in the clear water. I jumped onto the dock and found that I could just touch him by lying down and reaching over the edge.

I grabbed one of his arms and pulled. It was like trying to raise fifty kilos of wet paper. Even with the added buoyancy of the water, he was a heavy man for his size and he was doing little to help. Using all of my strength, I was able to lift him and drape his arms over the edge. After taking a breather, I wiggled and scraped him onto the dock. I was exhausted, but I knew I couldn't quit.

I rolled him over and listened for his breathing. He belched into my ear. He was drunk. I flopped down beside him. My heart was pounding from the exertion. My initial anxiety was subsiding and I began thinking of what I would do with Jake Lewis when I got back. In the distance, I could see the Supercub drifting toward the rocks.

The Supercub—I had forgotten about it! I had rescued the drunk without tying up. I dove in and wearily swam after it. I hauled myself on board and started the engine before the airplane could drift into the scrubby trees and rocks lining the shore. I set up my approach to the dock again and cut the power. My rescued friend was struggling to get up. He looked like a fat beetle stuck on its back. I tied the airplane securely.

"Good afternoon sir, are you Mr Mulligan?"

He giggled and nodded. It was obvious that he had spent his week at the cottage drinking.

My next problem was getting him into the airplane. He could stand only with my assistance. When I let go, he collapsed into a pile of giggles and belches. I half supported and half dragged him onto the airplane float, where I turned him around and let him fall backwards into the rear seat. He passed out. His legs were hanging outside, but there wasn't enough room to get behind and haul him in any farther.

One of the advantages of the Supercub was its Dutch door: the lower half swung down against the fuselage and the top part fastened under the wing. The airplane could be flown with the door open, so after doing up the old boozer's seat belt, I departed with his feet dangling outside.

At the time, the Airways pilots were paid three cents a kilometre for Supercub charter flights. For this sixty kilometre roundtrip, I could expect $1.80. Besides being wet and weary, I was peeved, but realized I would be out more than $1.80 if I lost Mr. Mulligan enroute. After takeoff, I periodically looked back to see if he was moving around.

Flying with the door open, the pilot is protected from the propellor slipstream by the windshield, but the passenger receives its full force. It didn't take long before the blast of fresh air revived Mr. Mulligan. He looked down over the side and threw up. The wind spread the residue over his shirt. Within seconds he passed out again.

He stayed out for the remainder of the flight, waking up after we landed. I didn't see him undo his seatbelt when I was concentrating on the docking. A few metres from the dock, his form slid by the corner of my eye into the bay.

Sam was standing ready to catch the airplane. His jaw dropped. He kept looking at the widening rings where Mr. Mulligan had disappeared and then back at me.

"Don't worry about it Sam, just get me the boat hook," I said, climbing out and tying up. Knowing Mulligan was drunk took some of the urgency out of the rescue.

The boat hook worked well. I pulled him over to the dock without jumping in. Sam and I were able to lie on our stomachs and drag him out of the water. There were no giggles this time. I think the large quantities of Georgian Bay he'd swallowed were sobering him up.

He sat on our dock for a long time declining any suggestions of an ambulance or hospital. When he could finally walk, he paid us from a waterlogged roll of bills, no tip. Then he got into his car and drove off.

Jake arrived from his last flight shortly after. His grin made it obvious that he had been waiting all day for this moment.

"How was Mr. Mulligan?"

He started to laugh before I could answer. I decided to get him where it would hurt the most, in the wallet, but it backfired.

"He was so drunk that he gave me a hundred dollar bill for a tip by mistake."

"Great! That means you're buying the beer. Let's go."

11/ SOLO ON THREE FINGERS?

I did eventually phone Pettigrew's list of prospects and slowly built up a handful of student pilots. My favorite was Bo Howard. Bo was a lean, tough guy in his mid-twenties with a beard and several tattoos carried over from five years in the Canadian navy. He had a good sense of humour and I enjoyed flying with him.

Bo had started learning to fly with the previous instructor. He was a good student, and I was able to continue his lessons with little review. I was planning to send him on his first solo flight during his next lesson if all went well. It was an easy decision to make with Bo because he was good at handling the airplane and seemed to be a street-wise character who could look after himself.

The lesson started typically enough with Bo phoning ahead. I took the call.

"It's Bo, my flight on for three o'clock?"

"Fine Bo, but that's in fifteen minutes. You'll never make it this time."

"I'll be there."

Bo worked at his family's marina at Rum Point, thirty kilometres north. To make it to his lesson on time, he had to flog his mother's clapped-out Oldsmobile 120 kilometres per hour along a two-lane highway clogged with a lethal summer mix of transport trucks and tourist trailers. The road was a continuous series of blind curves carved through walls of ancient Precambrian rock. No problem. At precisely three o'clock, Bo slid into our sandy parking lot in a cloud of dust with all four wheels locked up.

He got out of the car and ambled slowly into the office as if he had just walked from a house across the street.

"Lesson still on?"

Bo always arrived this way and he was never late.

I went with him first that day to make sure he was still flying well. I had not told him the ultimate objective of the lesson. The weather was calm and Bo made six good landings in a row. I told him to taxi to the dock for a full stop.

I climbed from the back seat onto the float, ready to assist his docking. It wasn't necessary. Bo's boating experience made the water handling the easiest part of his learning to fly. As we neared the wharf, I jumped from the float and grabbed the Supercub's wing strut. Then I turned and shoved the airplane off.

"Take her up for your first solo flight," I called across the widening gap to the Cub.

Bo wasn't there. I was talking to an empty airplane. He had anticipated my intentions and scrambled out of the pilot's seat while I was turning around. He was standing behind me.

"I don't want to go solo," he said sheepishly, in answer to the surprised look on my face.

I didn't know what to do. Nobody refuses to fly their first solo. "Why not?" I asked.

"I don't feel ready."

It wasn't the same Bo. The macho was all gone. I tried a little pressure. "I thought I was the instructor. I'm supposed to decide when you're ready and I say now."

He held up his right hand with one finger pointing up. "How many fingers?" he asked.

"One," I replied. I didn't see his point.

"Wrong. Three fingers: a navy buddy of mine showed up yesterday, and we had a three-fingered reunion. Right now I'm talking to three flying instructors and I'm telling them that I don't want to go solo."

"Okay, I get it, but you know what this means?"

"No."

"You have to swim for the plane," I said, indicating the drifting Cub.

He handed me his wallet and dove in. He swam to the Cub, climbed in and taxied back to the dock.

"In the pilot's shack you'll see three sofas. Why don't you pick one and sack out for a while? I'll fly a lesson with Dave Meeley. Then we can count fingers again and decide if you want to go flying."

"Okay," he said.

I was really just trying to keep him off the highway for a while. I didn't intend to fly with him again that day, but when I returned from my next lesson he was awake, drinking coffee with Beverly, and eager to fly.

"Can I go solo now?"

"No. Go home and we'll try it again next week." I didn't sound forceful enough.

"Give me the finger test. If I pass, I go solo, if not, I go home and come back hung over next week."

"Okay," I relented, "If you pass, I fly with you first to see if you can handle the Supercub sober."

"You gotta deal."

He passed the finger test and flew three good landings.

"Okay Bo, take her up."

His solo flight was flawless. I know because I watched it every step of the way. I approached him as he was tying up the plane afterward.

"Congratulations, Bo," I said, extending my hand.

He accepted it with a smile and a firm handshake. With one clean pull, I jerked him off balance, sending him across the narrow dock and into the bay on the other side. The first solo dunking was a float pilot tradition that I was eager to establish at Paradise. The idea lost some of its effect, since Bo was still damp when he went in, but I did it anyway. Fortunately for me, he came up smiling. He climbed out, extended a dripping right hand and said, "Thanks for having confidence in me."

I accepted his handshake, pleased that it had worked out. He jerked me off my feet and into the bay. I had both our wallets in my pockets. It didn't matter to Bo. The macho was back and he wanted me in the lake.

12/ THE YELLOW SUBMARINE

I think Pettigrew regretted promising to help Susan and me locate our little cottage by the water. We already knew that it wasn't going to be easy, and now he too was finding out. That was probably the reason he asked Henry to give me a Found checkout. He was being nice before welching on the accommodation. I didn't care. Upgrading to the Found meant more charter flights. After being wedged into the Supercub for three weeks, my enthusiasm for double fire patrols was wearing thin; I welcomed the change.

When I joined the staff, the Airways owned two Supercubs, two DeHavilland Beavers, a Cessna 180 and a Found. My students and I and a few rental pilots flew the Cubs. The other three pilots flew the Beavers and the Cessna 180. Nobody flew the Found. It had not occurred to me to ask why, but my first clue should have been Jake's nickname for the airplane, "The Yellow Submarine."

If I had asked, I might have been told that this was the Edsel of aircraft. It was the brainchild of two brothers named Found who set out to produce a four-place, Canadian airplane at Grand Bend, Ontario. It was conceived as a purpose-built bush plane, but it never lived up to the expectations of the designers or the operators. In a burst of marketing strategy, they called it the Found. Clifford Bannister bought two of the first models produced. His purchase was not based on a performance assessment, but on the fact that he had invested money in the Found Brothers' factory. Only a few operators followed his lead, so after a short production run, the Found slipped silently into history, but not before I spent a summer trying to fly it.

Henry started my checkout by supervising the pre-flight inspection. The airplane looked okay. It was a bit homely, but bush planes were not supposed to be pretty. Its slab sides and squared-off lines made it look like a streamlined woodbox, but the Found did have some unique features. To make it easier to load, the brothers eliminated the struts that on the Cessna 180 ran from the wings to the cabin, obstructing the doors.

The Found also beat the Cessna by having four doors. This allowed easy access to the entire cabin length for loading. The

Found was strong. The whole airplane appeared to be built like a tank. The fuselage was constructed from heavy one-inch-square tubing covered with aluminum. The thick wing skins had none of that flimsy oil-can look of the Cessna. The 250-horsepower, six- cylinder Lycoming engine was more powerful than anything I had flown. I was anxious to give it a try.

For the first time since he had checked me out in the Supercub, I could see that Henry was nervous. We had a long talk before we got in.

"See the railway bridge at the other end of the bay?" he asked.

"Yes." I was a bit puzzled because the bridge was a long way off and appeared to be only a few millimetres high, but I could see it.

"If you get everything right during the takeoff, we might clear that bridge. Just hope no train comes along."

"You're not serious."

"I'm as serious as a spinster on her first date."

"But we have a good breeze, only half fuel and two people."

"That's why I think we'll make it, if you get it right."

Henry then described what "getting it right" required.

"Start with half flap, full power and aim for the lighthouse."

"But that's forty-five degrees off the wind. I thought we were going to head for the bridge."

"We are. You aim for the lighthouse and the airplane will head for the bridge. The engine torque will make it turn. The curved take-off will give us more run, and you can see ahead through the left side window.

"There are a couple of other things you need to know. Make sure that your seatbelt is fastened and retract the flaps as soon as we're airborne. The throttle doesn't stay in, so I'll hold it for you. When you're solo, use your knee."

As we were getting ready to leave, I could see that a small crowd had gathered. In big cities, old guys hang around malls. In Paradise, they hung around the docks at the Airways. There were five of them watching us now. A green pilot's checkout in a new airplane was often their best form of entertainment. I didn't disappoint them.

I untied the lines to the dock and reached for the wing strut to keep the airplane from drifting away. There wasn't any wing strut. I grabbed at air and teetered on the edge of the dock. My arms were windmilling like an overweight hummingbird, but gravity was winning. I could see that I would have to swim to retrieve the airplane, so I gave up and fell in. The dock monkeys were all rocking on their heels with laughter. I ignored them as I stood waist deep in the lake and held the Found for Henry. At least the episode seemed to relieve some of his tension.

I pushed off and hopped into the pilot seat with a squish. The inside of the Found was pure bush. The floor and side panels were bare metal. The rear seat was just a canvas sling. The airplane had less upholstery than an army jeep, but like a jeep, the Found had a specific purpose. The sparse interior did not show the wear and tear from the rigors of bush loads. There was only one control wheel. The airplane did not have dual controls, and this was evidently the source of Henry's nervousness.

In the compromise world of aircraft design, the simple and strong Found had come out homely and overweight. The Found brothers had built a rugged bush plane that would barely fly. In an effort to lighten the airplane, they had removed all the sound-proofing, the rear seat and the second set of controls. Henry was a brave, or foolish, man.

When we were ready to go, I applied full power. The engine roared, and the nose came up. That was it. We were moving, but we didn't seem to be accelerating. For a long time the airplane struggled in the plow position with its long nose high in the air and prop spray blocking all forward view. It seemed like forever before I could feel that we were finally moving onto the step. Henry was right about the turning tendency. I held full right rudder, but the airplane swung steadily left. I looked out the side window, but if there had been any other waterborne traffic ahead, it would have been too bad. With the nose riding so high, it probably looked to local boaters like the airplane was departing with nobody on board.

On the step, I could feel the Found accelerate slowly. It was a good thing, because by now we were halfway to the bridge. We were rapidly running out of room when we broke free of the water's grip. It wasn't anything sudden, the spray off the floats just stopped. Then the airplane hung there without climbing. Henry pointed at the flap handle. In the Found it was an overhead mechanical lever between the pilots' heads. I reached up and released it as the shoreline filled the windshield.

In the rush and embarrassment of fishing myself from the lake, I had forgotten to fasten my seat belt. The strong upward motion of the released flap lever lifted me off my seat and pulled my hands and feet from the controls. The airplane started a diving turn towards the lake. I let go of the flap lever and hauled back on the wheel before Henry had time to do anything. Then I realized that there was nothing he could do. We cleared the bridge, but he wasn't grinning anymore.

Once the Found had built up some speed, it became a surprisingly well-mannered flying machine. Its extra weight and thick wings cushioned the afternoon turbulence, producing a smooth ride. The controls were heavy but predictable, and they gave the impression of flying a much larger airplane. After so many hours bobbing around in the little Supercub, I was starting to like this airplane.

Henry had said that my checkout would be just one circuit if I didn't do too badly. I was determined to make up for my takeoff by doing a good approach. I turned back toward the bay and reduced the power. It felt like we had been shot. Without the propellor thrust, the Found tucked her nose down and headed for the lake like a homesick whale. Henry didn't wait for my reaction. His huge hand engulfed mine on the throttle and he reapplied power to flatten the approach. He still wasn't grinning. The landing wasn't bad, but he made me do another circuit.

"We're not doing this for my sake," he said. "I could be sitting in the office drinking coffee, happy as a cat in a sandbox, so make this next one good."

I did.

I was determined to finish this checkout with the perfect docking just to regain some respect with the old groupies on the dock. Since they had been rewarded with my dunking at the beginning of the flight, they were still there. Float pilots are judged mostly by their docking. It is acceptable to take off in the wrong direction, get lost, bounce a landing or fall in the lake, as long as you execute a perfect docking.

Docking is difficult. A float pilot must estimate several changing conditions at the same time and shut the engine off, leaving enough way to steer the airplane on a curving approach to the slip. Too little speed and the wind swings the airplane around like a giant weathervane, pointing it toward whatever is in the way. This is followed by the pilot madly going through his engine restart procedure or, in tight quarters, digging out the paddle for his one-thousand-kilo canoe.

I had the opposite problem. I thought that I had judged it just right, but I hadn't counted on the extra weight of the Found. When I cut the power, nothing happened. The engine stopped, but the Yellow Submarine continued with the momentum of the *Queen Mary*. I wiggled the rudders in an attempt to kill some speed, but the airplane continued unabated into the slip.

The expressions on the bystanders' faces told the whole story. Their initial smirks changed to worry as they realized I was heading too fast for the dock on which they were standing. The worry spread to fear and the fear to panic as the Found charged the slip and mounted the low dock, accompanied by the sounds of protesting wood and floats.

They all managed to get clear, bumping into each other on the way. The airplane came to rest with one float on the dock and the other in the water. Henry was laughing. He knew that the only real damage would be to my ego. He had enjoyed watching the comic exit of the dock monkeys.

When he had regained his wind enough to speak, he said, "Next time come in from the other side, so the dock doesn't end up too far down the lake by the end of the summer."

13/ GEESE TALK

With my Found checkout, I became a patron of pet geese. The next Thursday, I drove to Saunder's Feedmill, bought a twenty-kilo sack of cracked corn, loaded it into the Found and flew to Lake George. The Cochrane family hunting cabin was on Lake George. Years ago, a great-uncle of this wealthy Toronto family had captured several Canada geese on the lake and clipped their wings so they couldn't fly. These birds became pets and required weekly feeding. Only a rich man like Uncle Cedric could explain the value of seeing the geese once a year. It was the Airways' job to keep them alive.

When I came to Paradise, the Cochranes had been paying for the cracked corn flights for years. I fed a growing number of freeloading descendants. Their wings weren't clipped, but they were too fat to fly. They seemed happy to live on the handouts. Pettigrew knew he was on to a good thing.

"Take the Found for the feed flight," he said.

"The grain sack would easily go in a Supercub." I replied.

"How much do we charge for the Supercub?" he asked.

"Thirty cents a kilometre."

"And the Found?"

"Fifty cents."

"That's why I'm the manager and you're the pilot. Take the Found."

Lake George was small and crescent shaped, with high, rocky shorelines, except where it dipped at one end to allow a creek to trickle in. Landing the Found there was no problem. I hugged the shoreline trees and reduced power. The airplane's steep glide allowed me to follow the high bank to the surface and touch down in a quarter of the lake's length. The water friction took over, and I stopped about midway around the curve.

I tied up at a rickety old dock jutting out from a thin strip of beach in front of the cabin. There were thirty to forty Canada geese of various sizes lined up along the sand like a welcoming committee. I was surprised by their size. The menacing beaks on the larger ones stretched nearly as high as my face. They were all hissing and honking impatiently.

As I unloaded the grain, their rising din echoed off the rock face on the far shore. I opened one corner of the bag and dragged it the length of the beach, trailing a row of cracked corn, as instructed by Henry. None of them ate. The largest bird was running up and down the line, flapping his wings and hissing a challenge to any who tried to feed. He was establishing his position as grand gander of the pecking order. Once satisfied he was going to eat first, he settled down and took some grain.

Another gander then erupted in a flurry of wings and beak, establishing his position as number two. This went on until the females decided number five gander was small enough that they would risk defiance. He was bowled over when the whole line rushed for the grain.

This trip was a pleasant break in the routine. The Cochranes had purchased all the land around the lake so the cabin sat by itself. There was no one around but the geese. I relaxed for a few minutes and watched the occasional skirmish break out along the food line.

When I was ready to go, I remembered Henry's warning that the Found was not ideally suited for departing Lake George. He assured me that I would make it, but there was only one way out. I would have to do a curving takeoff around the lake's kidney shape toward the creek.

The surface was dead calm because the high shorelines blocked the wind. I taxied into the far corner and applied full power. I had decided if I could get the airplane on the step before I caught sight of the dock, then there was sufficient room remaining to safely complete the takeoff. I plowed my way around the bend with the high-pitched whine of the propeller echoing off the rock walls. The dock came up too soon, way too soon. I cut the power to try again.

On the second attempt, I decided that I would have enough room to clear the trees if I could get on the step before I passed the dock. This time I turned around with the wingtip brushing the branches in the far corner. The second attempt was better. This was partly due to the roughing up the first pass had given the surface, making it easier for the floats to break loose. The dock flashed by just as the airplane struggled onto the step. I kept the power on, but as the long nose dropped, my first sight of the shoreline ahead scared me and I chickened out. At least the Yellow Submarine slowed quickly. The approaching trees didn't look so bad with the power off.

I had to give it one more try. It was either that or suffer the humility of being rescued by Henry. I decided that I still could make it by using the far end of the beach as my abort point. I shut down long enough to pump out the floats. This was a psychological move only, because the Found floats never leaked.

It worked. The third attempt was even better. It probably helped that I had burned off fuel in those two practise runs. The Found was accelerating well as I caught sight of the dock, but I saw something else – geese! The middle of the lake was now wall-to-wall waterfowl. Whether drawn by curiosity or by habit, the geese were taking an after-dinner swim across my departure path. The spectacle of the charging Found panicked the flock. They tried to scatter, but the best the overloaded birds could do was flap and paddle hard.

I cut the power as the Found's momentum carried me into their midst. I steered for a slowly widening space. I managed to miss them all, but I swamped a few with my wake.

It was obvious from all the beak waving that I was the target of the worst language geese could muster. I answered by swinging the airplane around and gunning the engine. I wanted to establish my dominance as grand gander on the water so I could gain a clear run for my fourth take-off attempt.

This time I was confident I could make it if the birds stayed out of the way. I wasted little time taxiing back and turning around in the corner. As I rounded the curve, I could see that the geese had not retreated completely to the shore, but had formed two ragged lines along my take-off path. The Found reached the step as I roared between them. From there, I hung on with my knee on the throttle and my hand on the flap lever in the blind faith that once this far the Found always made it. Besides, Henry had said it would. It was still close. Passengers would not have enjoyed climbing out between the trees along the winding creek.

I glanced back as soon as I dared. I could just see that the geese were having the last word.

14/ GYPSY MANSION

Pettigrew surprised me when he said that he had found us a cottage on a farm by a lake. I figured when he had offered his assistance, he was just paying lip service to pacify Susan. His announcement elevated my respect for him, but it didn't last.

"It won't be available until after Labour Day. The farmers have rented it to tourists during the summer, but they would be happy to have it occupied afterwards, at no charge."

"This is only May, Gary. Where do we stay between now and then?"

"The room next to Jake is available. You could stay there."

Jake lived on the third floor of the Queens Hotel. He liked it because the main floor of the old building was the town beer hall. I had been to Jake's room. It was decorated with a hundred layers of lead paint and peeling wallpaper. The fire escape was a hemp rope tied to a rusty radiator. The air conditioning was an open window.

"I don't think it's what Susan had in mind," I said.

"Well, I can't find anything else right now." The tone of his reply indicated that he wasn't going to try anymore either.

I told Bud Anderson my predicament. He was a new student pilot whose family ran a campground and cottage resort near town. He said, "The last flying instructor stayed at our place."

I already knew we could not afford one of the Andersons' cabins nestled on the hillside by the shore of Grove Lake. From Bud's tone, I thought maybe they had an unused apartment over the stables or a hut next to the septic bed, something unsuitable for tourists that was in our price range.

Then he added, "In a tent."

"Susan would die, but she would kill me first."

"You asked. It was just a suggestion. We have one site on top of the hill with no power or water. Dad would let you have it for half price on the season rate."

"Hello, Susan? Hi Honey. Listen, Mr. Pettigrew found us a pretty little cabin beside a beautiful lake right next to a wood and the owners will let us use it free just to keep it occupied."

56

I blew it; I had never called her 'Honey' before in my life.

"What's the catch?" she asked.

"We have to live in a tent for two months and a bit before we can have the cabin."

"How long?"

"Four months," but I knew I was making headway because she hadn't told me to get stuffed right off.

"Get stuffed."

I made it sound like a big adventure and promised her that we would do it in style. We would buy the biggest, most super deluxe tent offered by the Canadian Tire store. Besides, it seemed that we didn't have much choice.

She took a deep breath and said, "Yes."

We did it. It was one of those crazy things you do when you're young and broke. We sold most of our furniture and bought our gypsy mansion. It had two stand-up rooms with numerous pockets and zippers and several windows with little flaps and ties to keep the rain out.

I drove down the next week to pick her up. The girls where Susan had worked gave her a "camping shower" with all the 6-in-1 gadgets that she didn't have a clue how to operate. I took out the Volkswagon's rear seat and added a roof rack. When we started packing in everything we owned, our German Shepherd, Lady, pressed herself nervously against a fender, watching the limited space inside dwindle. We made it, but the car was so overloaded that the rear wheels splayed out like feet on a first-time ice skater. We headed north with the dog lying on top of the gear in the back, her panting grin filling the rearview mirror.

When I told Gary Pettigrew that we had found a place to stay, he asked for my phone number, "In case an emergency flight comes up on your day off."

To Gary, an emergency flight was one flight more than he had pilots for. I smiled and pointed to the top of the hill behind Grove Lake, "We don't have a phone, send smoke signals."

The only sour note in our little camping adventure was the end of the spring dry spell. It had started raining as we pulled into the campsite and continued off and on until Paradise recorded its wettest summer since they had started keeping track of such things. Everything was waterlogged. Our camping neighbours knew when I was home from work by the whoosh of gasoline exploding; it was the only way to light the campfire.

Susan developed permanently chapped rings around her legs from wearing shorts and rubber boots, and the tent always smelled of damp dog. When the mold grew up the inside of the canvas walls she said, "Don't you ever try and 'Honey' me again."

15/ TWO FOR ONE

The rain brought foggy mornings. At first light, the Saturday following Susan's move, I sat in the office with the other three pilots drinking the shellac we called coffee. The airplanes rested expectantly in
their slips. We were waiting for the weather to improve, remembering the warm beds we had left needlessly an hour ago. The rain had
cancelled out the fire patrols, but it didn't mean less work. The bad
weather compressed the charter flights into whatever flying hours
we could get. I had been flying the Found regularly all week and enjoying it. We were savoring this respite granted by the fog before
starting another busy day; then Pettigrew bustled in.

He peered anxiously at the full booking sheet, knowing his life
would quickly become complicated if there were further delays.
Gary's previous job had been running the Bannister Family Discount Store. Nobody knew why he was hired to manage the Airways or why he would want to. Gary had no flying experience and
was afraid to climb a low stool. He was constantly worried about
being chewed out by Bannister, because Bannister frequently
chewed him out. An ever-present glass of milk in his hand was testi-
mony to the havoc that the job raised in his stomach.

As newest man on the pilot roster, I was the first pilot he approached. "Looks like a full schedule today; are you going to be able
to get your first customer out soon?"

My reply was according to one of Henry's unwritten rules. In
bad weather, the chief pilot goes first. "I don't know," I said, "you'll
have to ask Henry."

He shuffled over to the big man and asked hopefully, "Henry,
when do you think you'll be able to start these trips?"

Henry smiled his friendly, tobacco-stained smile and pointed out
the window, "See that ridge out there across the bay?"

"No."

"Well, neither do I, but when I do, then maybe we'll start flying.
You watch the ridge and tell me when you see it."

The airplanes we flew had basic instrumentation, but the windshield was our main reference. Since we seldom flew far, we knew

58

the area well enough to safely fly in minimal visual conditions, but we did have to see where we were going. The ridge in question was Henry's weather indicator. It was about two kilometres away and was the highest point of land in the area. When Henry could see it, he knew he could clear any obstructions for a wide radius. Risking passengers and aircraft for the sake of staying on schedule was not acceptable to Henry. It was difficult and expensive to replace a crashed airplane during the busy season, but his major concern was the passengers. "Killing customers is bad for business" was one of his favorite expressions.

Gary accepted the soundness of the philosophy, but he fussed anyway. This morning he frequently darted out of his office to peer into the gloom for a glimpse of Henry's ridge. He knew that the phone would soon ring, and Bannister would demand to know why he wasn't hearing any aircraft engines from his house on the hill. Despite this, nobody tried to force me to fly until Henry said it was good enough.

The customers didn't mind the delay. They had their first beers open and were starting their vacations right in our hangar. My own customer that foggy morning was using the air service for the first time. Gordon MacDougall was a self-professed, part-time hermit. He was a tough little man who strutted about with a no-nonsense air that reminded me of a high school shop teacher. He told me that he lived in an apartment building in Toronto and worked for the city. He came north every chance he could get to spend time alone in his cottage.

While we waited, Mr. MacDougall talked. "I normally drive my Morris Minor to the marina at the other end of my lake and then go the last five kilometres by motorboat. When I come to town for supplies, I often stop by here to watch the airplanes. I decided someday to give it a try as a little adventure for myself. So here I am."

MacDougall didn't mind waiting for the fog to lift. He had never been in an airplane before and was enjoying being part of the goings-on at the Airways. He considered the delay a bonus.

Normally we flew customers to their cottages and returned empty. At the end of their stay we would fly back empty and pick them up. This seemed dreadfully cost-inefficient to MacDougall, so he had arranged just one flight. I was to fly him to his cottage, drop off his gear and then he was going to fly back to town with me to pick up his car, finishing the trip his normal way. This gave him two airplane rides for the price of one and avoided the cost of another roundtrip flight to bring him out. MacDougall's cottage was on the long arm of a large lake and his load was light, so it was a good trip for the Found.

When the weather improved, Henry took off first. MacDougall and I climbed into the Found with his gear. We listened to the radio for Henry to tell us if it was clearing on the other side of the ridge. MacDougall was interested in all the cockpit dials and switches, so I used the time to explain their functions.

Henry's voice boomed through my headset. He always yelled on the radio because he didn't trust electricity to do the amplifying for him. "The weather on the other side of the ridge is like the weather on your side of the ridge. It'll be dandy if everyone stays low without hitting anything." Then, just to bug Pettigrew a little, he added, "Looks like we might have started sooner."

I signalled to Sam to cast us off and started the ritual of looking for a clear run through the scattered boat traffic. We were next to depart in the reduced visibility, because the Found was faster than the airplanes the other two were flying. The Yellow Submarine's endless take off was somewhat shorter thanks to MacDougall's small amount of gear and a boat wake that helped launch us into the air.

I had never been to MacDougall's lake before, so I did a slow pass over his section before landing. His face lit up when he saw his place from the air for the first time. I inspected the long bay for rocks, logs and wire crossings, while MacDougall checked out what his neighbours were doing to their cottages. The dark water looked deep and clear that calm, grey morning, and I could see no obstructions. I set up an approach toward the end of the bay and stopped close to MacDougall's dock.

We unloaded his things and reboarded for the return flight. It was an easy takeoff. There was no boat traffic, the airplane was light and I had the entire length of the bay and four kilometres of lake beyond. Conversation in flight was impossible, but I pointed out some of the local landmarks as we flew back to Paradise.

MacDougall thanked me for showing him a good time when we were taxiing to the dock after landing. He was visibly excited by the flight. "I always wondered if the pilot would fly under or over the wires crossing the bay when I took a plane into my place," he said.

I didn't reply, as I felt the colour drain from my face. There were no wires crossing MacDougall's bay. At least I hadn't seen any.

I contemplated how close we might have come to snagging hydro lines in flight. We must have passed the wires on both the landing and the takeoff. An airplane as heavy as the Found may have been able to break a small hydro service wire, but the heavier high-voltage transmission lines have been known to stop larger airplanes in flight, zap them to a crisp and then drop the remains into the drink.

Shivering at the thought, I forgot to cut the power early while docking the Found. We charged the dock so hard that I sent Sam running for cover. The airplane mounted the planks with both floats and stopped at a crazy angle, almost clean out of the water.

MacDougall said nothing but smiled nervously as he climbed

down and scurried off to his Morris. Sam helped me horse the Found back into the lake. I used half my lunch to bribe him not to tell his dad about my absentminded arrival. I was more concerned about my absentminded flying.

Gordon MacDougall is the only one who will ever know how close we came, but he is probably never going to fly again, because he thinks the most dangerous part of his trip was our slamming into the dock.

16/ RECOMMENDED

The weather stayed down for most of June. The low clouds and occasional rain forced us to "scud run" our flights. To maintain ground contact, we flew low over the lakes and river valleys, weaving around the shredded bits of lower clouds. I was getting used to it. The worst flying was in the evening when the temperature dipped and so did the clouds.

That was the situation when I dropped a passenger off at Happy Harbour in the Supercub. I headed for home. The clouds were settling. It looked like I had tried to complete one too many trips that day. I decided to fly along the Trans Canada Highway. I was low. I throttled back and settled in behind a transport truck, keeping my floats just above and behind his trailer. I followed him through the highway cuts in the rock and trees for twenty minutes. I doubt he knew I was there, unless his mirror was angled up. It must have looked funny to the traffic coming the other way. This was not the kind of flying everyone would enjoy, but I was familiar with the terrain and could always land at the next lake.

I realized that the clouds were too low for me to make it over Henry's ridge, just before our base. Jake had told me about a good place to land for the night just south of there.

"If you can't get over the ridge, land on the lake behind the Ramsey House Restaurant and Tavern on the highway. Then call me, I'll drive down and pick you up."

It wasn't far now, but I was scraping the underside of the clouds. I couldn't fly any lower because of oncoming trucks. I had already decided to land at the next lake when I recognized the restaurant as we rounded a bend. I banked right, cut the power and dropped onto the water.

There was a dock behind the building, but no one was around. I tied up and walked in the back door. A few kitchen staff were busy getting ready for the supper crowd. I asked to use a phone.

"In the bar," one of them said, pointing down a hallway.

The bar was deserted except for a big guy cleaning glasses behind the counter. "Hi. Where did you come from?" he asked in a booming voice.

"I just landed in a floatplane out back. Is it all right if I leave it there for the night and use your phone?"

"Sure, no problem. Help yourself. Are you one of the pilots from the Airways?"

"Yes sir," I replied.

It turned out that the bartender was George Popoluk, the owner of Ramsey House. George was a friendly giant of a man. He told me that he was interested in aviation.

"I even took some lessons when I lived in Hamilton, years back. Sit down and have a beer, on the house. Looks like you're done flying for the day."

I accepted his offer, and we talked airplanes for some time before I realized that the office would be waiting to hear from me.

"Hi Beverly, I'm secure for the night just down the highway. Is Jake there?"

"Hi Jake, I'm at the Ramsey House. Ten minutes, thanks, see you then."

"Have another beer while you're waiting." George was already pouring it before I could accept.

We talked about flying some more and then George said, "I've been thinking about finishing my pilot licence at the Airways, but I hear the new instructor came with no float experience. What do you think? Is the guy any good?"

Now, I don't like people putting one over on me, but George left himself wide open, and after two beers, I couldn't resist.

"I wouldn't worry about his float time. What he lacks in experience he makes up with his natural ability. I think you'd find him a first-rate instructor."

"That could be, but I don't want to fly with a hot-shot rookie. I think I'll wait and meet him later in the summer."

My ears started to burn. It was as if George had watched me fly up the highway a few minutes ago and knew I'd been showing off. Jake's arrival saved me from having to reply.

"George, you old bear; how ya doin'?"

"Jake, my favorite grounded pilot; did you land out back too?"

"Not this time, I came to collect my lost friend here."

"Stay for a beer anyway? On the house."

"George, you are a gentleman and a scholar; how can I refuse?"

Apparently Jake had discovered George's hospitality some time ago and landed there at the slightest hint of bad weather near the end of the day. Free beers for anyone who would talk about flying, that was heaven to Jake.

I decided to get a little back at George for unknowingly referring to me as a hot-shot rookie. "Jake, George was asking me about our new flying instructor. I told him the man was top notch. What do you think?"

Jake looked puzzled, but he caught on quickly. "The new guy, oh yes; the best, a true ace, George."

"But Jake, you said to wait until the new pilot either killed himself or learned to avoid taking chances."

Jake didn't hesitate for a minute. "Ah, but George, that was before I had a chance to show him the ropes. Now that I've taught him the tricks of the trade, he's become an excellent pilot, you'll see."

It was much later before the bull stopped flying and we headed for home. By the time I got to the tent it was dark and the macaroni and cheese Susan had made for my dinner had solidified into one lump. I went to bed hungry, a little more humble and more than a little drunk. I wondered what George would say when he met the new instructor.

17/ PLAY STABLE

Susan lasted two wet days in the tent with the damp dog. Then she ventured out to make the most of her holidays in rainy Paradise. An hour later, she had seen all there was to see of the area through the fogged-up windows of the Volkswagen, but she had found what she was looking for, the local stables. Susan had been interested in horses since childhood.

Mason Stables was located a few miles south of town. It was a family operation run by Pamela and Duncan Mason and their daughter Margaret. The Masons were likeable transplanted Brits whose main business was taking tourists out for trail rides. Susan went riding, every day, in the rain. Since she was their only customer during the miserable weather, the Masons were very nice to her. They asked her into the house each time and offered her a towel and tea. They would chat a few hours away, before Susan returned to the soggy misery of our tent. I was relieved that she found something to do, because I loved the bush flying and I was afraid it would end if she got fed up.

It was during one of her chats with Pamela Mason that Susan asked for a job. The suggestion took Pamela by surprise. Susan's designer blue jeans and the way she handled conversation and a teacup told Pamela that it was not Susan's station in life to muck out stalls. At least not where Pamela came from, but she was tempted. Her husband worked at the Bannister Lumber Mill in town and helped when he could. The rest of the time she relied on her daughter and a few young girls to take out the rides and look after the care and feeding of twenty horses. Susan represented the opportunity to hire a responsible adult, but she had to watch her dollars. Most of the stable's income came during the short summer season and the horses had to be fed year 'round.

She took a chance. "I'll take you on, but I can only pay you $5 a day."

"Does that include lunch?" That was my girl. Feed her and she would follow you anywhere.

"Lunch included."

"Fine; I'll take it."

The job got Susan out of the tent. It meant one less meal for her to cook over our temperamental camp stove and all the riding and shovelling she would ever want. What more could a fashion buyer desire?

That night she told me about it over supper.

"I got a job today."

"Fantastic. I didn't even know you were looking." I really was excited. At the time, I was eating macaroni and cheese again, and her announcement brought visions of our former life of dual incomes and good meals.

"At Bannister's Family Discount?" I asked.

"No, I decided that I didn't want to go back to my salesgirl days, so I found something completely different."

The vision was fading a little. Susan wasn't trained for anything else, but I remained optimistic. "What did you find?"

"I'm working for the Masons at the stables for $5 a day and all I can eat."

Now it was my turn to be surprised, but what could I say? Since I had accepted the Airways job without discussing it first, I certainly couldn't complain about her taking this one without telling me. I didn't have any right to suggest that she should be making more money, so I said, "Would it be possible for you to bring home some of your lunches for me?"

"No way; you never brought me home smoked salmon from the Westleys. You'll just have to arrange more mealtime lessons with Ian."

I went to see the stables on my next day off. It was unbelievable. Duncan Mason had built the house and the barn himself, entirely out of scraps from the Bannister Lumber Mill. Both buildings were constructed with beautifully varnished, tongue and groove pine, but not one piece was longer than half a metre. The short boards made the place look like a Fisher-Price play stable, but that added to its charm. Whenever a horse kicked or chewed a board, Duncan easily snapped in another small piece. Pamela Mason cooked on a wood stove fueled by Bannister scraps, and the horses were bedded down in wood shavings from the mill.

Susan loved working there. I should have been paying Pamela Mason the $5 a day. The job probably saved my hide. Without it, Susan would not have lasted long in the tent that rainy summer. She mucked stalls and led trail rides, taking our German Shepherd with her. Before long, the two of them were in better physical and mental condition than ever, and I was able to keep flying at the Airways.

18/   SEVENTY-FIVE PERCENT

In the middle of June, I moved up. The staff remained the same, but Pettigrew asked Henry to check me out in the Cessna 180. I wasn't doing many fire patrols in the off-and-on rain, but the charter business was picking up. The only time I could help out with the Found was on the odd trip into a long lake. If there was a load to come out and I could see the other end of the lake, then it wasn't long enough.

Len Willard, the other Airways pilot, usually flew the One-Eighty. At nineteen, Len was younger than I, but he had learned to fly on floats at his hometown of Orillia, Ontario. He was tall, handsome and confident. Our passengers didn't mind flying with Len because he looked much older. He seldom spoke, which added to his mature bush pilot image. Len filled in on a Beaver whenever Jake or Henry was off. That was when I would fly the Cessna.

My checkout was simple. Henry stood beside the plane and said, "Do you remember flying the Found?"

"Yes, I flew it this morning."

"Good. Now remember 75 percent."

"Okay, 75 percent," I replied. I had already learned not to question the way Henry approached things. He always got to the point; it just took a little longer. Asking questions made it a lot longer. "To fly the Cessna, just remember 75 percent of the Found. The Cessna carries 75 percent more weight than the Found, but takes 75 percent longer to load and unload. It takes off in 75 percent of the distance, at 75 percent of the speed. It cruises 75 percent slower, burning 75 percent of the gas. Approach speed, stall speed and landing distance are all 75 percent. Got that?"

"I think so."

"Good, then take it up for a few circuits." He started to walk away.

"Aren't you coming with me?"

"No. It doesn't have dual controls. If you need me, I don't wanna be there. If you don't need me, then I don't need to be there. In either case, I'm going to be in the pilot shack drinkin' coffee. It's 75 percent easier to fly than the Found and you haven't killed yourself in that, so you won't have any trouble." He was right. The Cessna was easier to fly. It had less horsepower (75 percent), but was much lighter. The airplane was basically a big empty soup can with wings on top and an engine in front. It wasn't really designed for Canadian bush work, so it was difficult to load and the metalwork cracked constantly from the pounding on floats and skis.

For my self-directed checkout, I visited a couple of small lakes that were tight for the Found, including the geese on Lake George. The Cessna's performance was mediocre when compared to a Super-cub, but it beat the Found flaps down.

19/ DAMAGE CONTROL

My first revenue flight in the Cessna 180 was to the French River. This was just north of the Pickerel River, in the same area of smooth rock and clean water. The week before, a retired American couple in a fancy cruiser had tied up at the Bannister Marina. Their son and his wife had joined them there for a week of cruising Georgian Bay. They arranged for the Airways to pick up the younger couple at the French River and fly them back to their car in Paradise.

I had a map with the pre-arranged spot marked on it. There weren't many trees along this part of the river and the white cruiser stood out big as a house. I couldn't miss it. It was anchored in a long, narrow section, perfectly suited for the Cessna. I landed into the wind and coasted to a stop. The wing would not fit over the boat, but they had already thought of that. Dad loaded his son and daughter-in-law into a rubber dinghy and motored them the short distance to the plane. I stood on the float and helped them on board.

The girl sat beside me with her husband behind. She was nervous. I tried some idle chatter to settle her down.

"Is this your first time in a small plane?" I asked.

"Yes," she replied.

"Well, you're really going to enjoy it. It's more fun than the airlines."

The river was about thirty metres wide at this point. I taxied past the cruiser to get enough room to turn around. I needed to backtrack downstream, downwind before taking off. I increased power and applied full left rudder for the turn. The airplane was slow to respond against its weathercocking tendency. I added more power. It took the full width, but it did come around. In fact, it continued around to the left, back into the wind. We were now headed at the cruiser.

I had forgotten to lower the water rudders after landing. Without them, I was at the mercy of the wind. The old couple on the boat had been smiling and waving their good-byes until it became obvious that we were going to hit them. There was a split second when I considered full power. The propellor blast against left rudder might have tightened the turn upwind enough to miss the cruiser. But I decided against it, because I didn't like the thought of 2700 RPM chew-

69

ing into the side of the boat.

The girl was screaming and her husband was gripping the back of her seat. I held left rudder and killed the engine. As it was, we almost made it. The wind continued to weathercock the airplane upstream. The right wing tip swiped the railing on the boat's bridge.

I was afraid if I stopped to survey the damage the girl would jump into the river, dress and all, and refuse to get back in. I could see the wires from the navigation light hanging from the wing tip, but that appeared to be the only damage. I decided to take off.

We drifted clear of the cruiser, and I immediately fired up the engine. The girl's screams had subsided into sobs.

"Not a good way to start a first flight," I mumbled lamely.

Now I had to execute the turn all over again, but this time I did it with the water rudders down. No problem.

I had thirty minutes on the flight back to Paradise to worry about the consequences of my stupidity and subsequent decision to fly the damaged airplane. I thought I knew Henry well enough to count on a long safety monologue for flying with a broken nav light. I was more worried about Pettigrew's reaction.

I figured the manager would applaud my completing a revenue flight, but he had a policy of withholding one cent per kilometre of our salary against damage. The penny was considered a bonus to be paid at the year end to any pilot who did not damage an airplane. I didn't mind paying for a new nav light, but I already had $100 in my bonus fund and I didn't want to lose it. If I had to forfeit a whole year's bonus, maybe I should quit right now.

The trip had been prepaid, so the young couple immediately got in their car and drove off, saving me any more embarrassing apologies. I went straight to Pettigrew's office. He was drinking a glass of milk.

"Gary, I smashed up the One-Eighty."

I should have waited until he swallowed. He choked and sprayed milk all over his desk.

When he had recovered enough to speak, he said, "Where is it?"

"It's here. I flew it back damaged."

"You what!"

"I flew it back damaged. Come see for yourself."

He stood on the dock, looking it all over and finally said, "I don't see any damage."

"I know. It's on the other side."

We turned the airplane around in its slip, and I pointed to the missing nav light.

"That's not what I call smashing up an airplane," he said angrily.

Those were the sweetest words that he could have uttered.

"Would you care to put that in writing, Gary? I'm a little afraid of my bonus."

"No, I won't put it in writing, and if you ever scare me like that again, you won't get any bonus." He stormed back to the office to find more milk.

I went to the maintenance hangar and told the mechanics about the damaged Cessna. Ken Noonan was ecstatic. Ken was the Airways' chief mechanic. He and his apprentice, Chico Sanchez, were always happy to find a bent airplane. When they didn't have any aircraft maintenance, they were under standing orders to fix a lineup of broken stoves and refrigerators brought in from Bannister Propane Rentals. They also maintained the school buses for Bannister Bus Lines (that explained the bright yellow paint on the airplanes), and they were on standby to drive the local ambulance that was always parked beside the hangar (Bannister Ambulance—bright red paint). But their first love was repairing airplanes.

Ken was a happy, fun-loving guy. He was the one who stencilled "Fly Yellow Side Up" on the Supercub. I told him about swiping the side of the cruiser, and he laughed. I told him about the girl screaming, and he laughed harder. I told him Pettigrew's reaction when I said that I had smashed up the plane, and Ken had to sit down to keep from falling over with laughter. His ability to see the funny side of everything made me feel better.

I went looking for Henry. Since he had trained me, I felt that I had let him down. I wanted to tell him about the incident before someone else did. I was too late.

He was in the pilot shack bent over the Beaver's radio. Henry hated talking into a microphone, but he loved taking radios apart. When I walked in, he said, "I hear you did a modification to the One-Eighty."

"Yes sir. I was hoping to tell you myself."

"Gary's pretty quick to tell me that a pilot's gone wrong," he said. "I guess I should've warned you the Found wingspan is 75 percent less than the One-Eighty."

"No sir. I forgot to lower the water rudders," I said nervously.

"Well, you'll know better next time. Every pilot needs a good scare to settle him down. If this was yours, you got off lucky."

"Yes sir," I said, bracing myself for a long lecture.

He turned back to working on the radio. After an awkward silence I blurted out, "Is that it?"

He looked a little surprised. "Yes. What did you expect?"

"Well, I thought you'd give me more of a lecture," I said, looking at the floor.

"Pettigrew is the one who cries over spilled milk, so don't get me started.

"Yes sir," I replied.

As I made to leave, he said, "There is one more thing."

"Yes sir?"

"My name is still Henry."

"Thanks, Henry."

20/ THE LOST FOUND

Ken Noonan and his wife, Joy, invited Susan and me over for dinner out of sympathy for the tent people. Their small-town hospitality was welcome, and the four of us became good friends. Saturday dinner at the Noonans became a regular event. Ken and Joy treated us to the typical Paradise weekend entertainment: playing cards over a few drinks and watching *The Amazing Kreskin*, CBC's summertime replacement for *Hockey Night In Canada*.

One evening Ken told us the story of what happened to the Airways' second Found. "Three years ago, Gary Pettigrew placed ads for a Found pilot in several magazines. He picked the best prospect from all the replies and invited him for an interview. The new fellow had bush experience in Cessna 180s, so Gary decided Henry should take him flying to see how he handled the Found. Gary left the office to look for Henry in the pilot shack.

"Meanwhile, another hopeful arrived, uninvited. He asked Beverly about the job. This guy had no time. The ink was still wet on his commercial pilot licence, and he had never been in a floatplane. His name was Norbert Schumacher. Beverly asked him to wait for the manager, who was interviewing another candidate."

Ken started chuckling just thinking about the story.

"Gary found Henry out back and told him to grab the guy in the office and take him up in a Found. While waiting, the first guy went to the bathroom. It cost him the job.

"Henry stuck his head in the door and yelled, 'Hey you, let's go.'

"This guy Norbert obediently followed Henry down to the dock. They stood beside the Found looking at each other. Henry pointed to the airplane and said again, 'Well, let's go.'

"Norbert was keen, but he had never touched a floatplane before. Henry became a little suspicious when he hopped in and closed the door with the Found still tied to the dock. He shrugged it off, knowing Gary had done worse before. With help from Henry, the Norbert fella got the airplane untied and fired up." Ken laughed.

"I don't know how he got the Found airborne, but he did, and he brought it around for an approach without alarming Henry too much.

"From the right seat, Henry had as much control over his flight as a baby kangaroo. He was helpless except for gesturing and shouting over the engine noise.

"Norbert lined up for the bay and cut the power off completely. The Found dropped like a broken elevator. Norbert froze at the controls. Henry added power by reaching across, but it wasn't enough. The airplane struck the lake in shallow water at a forty-five-degree angle and went straight to the bottom."

Ken imitated Henry hopelessly gesturing as the airplane went down. We were all laughing so hard I was afraid that Ken wouldn't be able to finish the story.

"The Found was a write-off, but it remained intact. Both pilots were able to open their doors and swim to the surface. If they had been in any other airplane, they'd be dead.

"With that machine gone, we didn't need another pilot, so both new guys got the boot before they were hired. Henry went into Gary's office still dripping wet and told him what he thought of his pilot selection process."

Ken showed us a picture of the wreck before they pulled it out of the water. All that appeared above the surface was a small triangle of rudder. It became a parts airplane for the sister ship, which survived several more pilots at the Airways, including me.

21/ PADDLE WARRIOR'S REVENGE

When it rained on a Thursday, I discovered why the other pilots didn't like feeding the geese. The low cloud and poor visibility that day backed up the schedule. Pettigrew had worn a path in the linoleum between his office and the window before Henry could see his ridge well enough to take the first trip out. I automatically postponed the feed flight until Friday.

I didn't think the geese would notice the extra day. I was wrong. When I tied up to the dock, several of the larger ganders waddled up the planking. They approached me with mouths open and wings flapping. I was late and they knew it, and they wanted me to know they knew it.

I turned to haul the grain from the airplane. The lead gander lunged and bit me in the rear. I yelped and swung around with the twenty-kilo sack in my arms. He bit my knee, hard. I dropped the corn, jumped into the airplane and closed the door.

I understood then why some people kept a few geese in their yard instead of Dobermans. The bites through my jeans raised welts that took days to heal. I squirmed to find a comfortable side to sit on and contemplated what to do next. The angry birds on the dock showed no signs of retreating. I considered leaving and letting them try and figure out how to undo burlap stitching on their own. As the initial pain subsided, I decided I couldn't let a few birds defeat me.

What worked in the end was a swinging paddle. I charged out of the airplane like Custer during his last stand. I dragged the heavy bag with one hand and swung the paddle with the other. A couple of geese were knocked flying into the lake, and I suffered a few more nips, but I gained the beach. I opened the bag, dumped the grain in a single pile and ran back to the airplane. Some of my humour was restored when I saw the chaos created by thirty birds trying to eat from one mound.

I got my revenge by using Lake George as a training ground. I took each of my students to visit the geese at least once during their float training. It worked well. The lake was hard to find because it was recessed into the forest, and the rock-faced shorelines made it look more intimidating than it was. There were no cottagers for us to harass with repeated practise and no boaters to bother us. The lake was tight for an empty Found, but just right for a loaded Super-cub. The student pilots thought that I was just showing them short field work, but the main purpose of our visit was to confuse the geese. When the flock saw the red and yellow airplane land, they would line up expectantly on the beach. I smiled to myself each time we took off without leaving grain.

It worked. I don't really know if it was the training flights throwing them off or their respect for the paddle warrior, but the gaggle always stayed on the beach whenever I brought grain.

22/ JAKE

It is an unwritten law of the bush that the pilots keep their customers' empty beer bottles. Just ask any passenger who has tried to take them home. At the Airways, the pilots pooled their bottles. Sam would store the empties in the hangar until Friday, when he would use Ken Noonan's pickup truck for a run to the Brewers' Retail store. At the height of the summer, we would average ten cases a day. At five cents a bottle for the returns, we could clear nearly $100 a week. Ken looked after the money. Half of it went to local community work. One week it would be donated to the Boy Scouts, the next to a needy family that Ken had met through his ambulance driving, and so on.

The other half we drank. Friday was our party night at the Queens Hotel. Our weekly gathering included Ken, Chico, Sam, Jake, Len, the guys from Bannister Propane and Bannister Marina, and cable TV man Oscar Fleming. Henry always declined, and we never invited Pettigrew.

I felt guilty leaving Susan in the damp tent that night, but I had developed a good friendship with the group before she moved to Paradise and I hated to give it up. She was a good sport and never asked me to.

Jake Lewis was usually the centre of attention at the party. Jake always told a good story on himself, as he frequently found himself in laughable situations. One Friday he told us about a trip that he had messed up that very day. He was supposed to have flown a customer to Toronto, but he missed it, by two hundred kilometres.

"Everything looks the same down there," he moaned.

"Come on Jake," I said, "Southern Ontario is a map-reading paradise. There are roads, railroads, rivers, powerlines and cities everywhere. Up here, there are only rocks, water and trees."

"That's why it's impossible to navigate there. The roads are all going in the same direction and every mother-loving town has a railroad, a powerline and a river. They're all identical. Up here, each shoreline is different."

"What is Toronto identical to?" I asked.

"I didn't see it."

Whenever we flew to Southern Ontario, our destination was always Toronto. The floatplane dock beside the Toronto Island Airport was a short ferry ride away from a metropolitan core of 3 million people. Jake had made the trip before.

"Since the map is no good, I always fly south and wait 'til I hit Lake Ontario. Then I turn left or right; I have a 50/50 chance of being right. If I don't recognize something soon, I go the other way."

Jake was a good bush pilot, but flying to Toronto did not qualify as a bush flight, so he got lost. A strong northeasterly wind messed up his navigation. The trip to Toronto Island was about an hour in the Found. His "fly south" method would have worked except Lake Ontario ended at Hamilton, fifty kilometres west of Toronto. Jake missed Lake Ontario altogether.

"I thought the strong wind was slowing us down, so I just kept on trucking. The customer, Mr. Big City, was in a hurry and looked at his watch a lot. I just smiled at him; I knew what I was doing."

Jake would have kept going until he ran out of gas in the mountains of West Virginia, except that he came to Lake Erie, the next lake in the Great Lakes chain. He thought it was Lake Ontario.

"I saw Oshawa and I knew I was home free. I smiled at my passenger again and turned right."

He should have turned left. The town he had seen was really Port Dover. Then he headed further west.

"After a while, Mr. Big City got agitated again. I told him to relax. I couldn't see Toronto yet, but we were running out of gas. I saw a marina, so I landed to refuel. I asked a guy how much further to Toronto. I almost fell over when he said, 'two hundred kilometres,' and then he pointed in the wrong direction. My passenger was really upset."

Jake had landed at Port Burwell, south of London, Ontario. When he took off, this time going the right way, he was flying straight into the teeth of the strong wind.

"An hour later, we were low on fuel again. I hadn't filled up completely at the last place, because they only had low-octane boat gas. I thought the customer was going to go berserk. He was jumping up and down in his seat and swearing a blue streak at me. I told him that I didn't have to take that kind of abuse and he could get out anytime. I landed at Hamilton and never saw him again. I don't know why he was in such a knot."

By then, Jake had flown three hours, about the time it takes to drive from Paradise to Toronto. Since he didn't have a passenger anymore, he flew home. It was against the wind, so he had to add more boat gas at Midland, but he didn't get lost.

His passenger took a cab home from Hamilton and reamed out Pettigrew on the phone before Jake got back. He demanded his money back plus cab fare for the waste of time and swore he would never fly with us again.

When Gary tried to pass this hostility on to Jake, he replied, "I don't know why you're so upset Gary, the man had no patience."

Len joined our party that night from a late charter flight, after Jake had finished telling us the story.

"How was Toronto, Jake?" he asked.

"It's not there. Have a beer, and I'll tell you about it."

23/ DOODLEBUGS AND THE ENGLISHMAN

"Say sport, could ya point out the best fishing spots on this lake on the way in?"

The question came from my back seat passenger in the Found. He had leaned forward and stuck his face in my ear to be heard over the engine noise. I was assaulted by a wave of secondhand beer fumes. I was flying this angler and his buddy into a fishing camp on Wauwaskesh Lake.

"Sure, I'd be glad to," I yelled in reply.

"Thanks pal. Say, what lures are they usin' for lake trout here?"

"Let's see what you've got." I was learning.

The people in this world can be separated into two distinct groups: the ones who love fishing with a passion and the rest. Most of the rest consider fishing as exciting as watching paint dry. I belong to that second group. I don't even like eating seafood. I didn't think fishing had anything to do with being a good bush pilot. I was wrong.

When I started charter flying, I answered my passengers' fishing questions by saying, "I don't know; I don't like fishing."

It wasn't the right thing to say. Passionate anglers do not understand that there are some people who don't believe heaven is a lake full of hungry trophy fish. Americans spending big dollars for a few days casting in remote Canadian lakes want their pilots to love fishing.

Next I tried bluffing. If I saw a boat in the lake, I'd point that out as the ideal spot. I would pick the most colourful lures in the customer's tackle box and tell them to use those. I didn't think it made much difference. It did.

I was sending fishermen with deep sea lures into weed beds and they didn't appreciate it. Clyde Morrison, the Wauwaskesh Fishing Lodge owner, straightened me out. It didn't take him long to find where his customers were getting all the dumb information. He took me aside one day and firmly suggested that I educate myself.

"Do me a favor and ask your homebound passengers where the fish were hitting and what lures worked. After a while you'll get an idea of what's happening. In the meantime don't say anything. I'll tell them where to go and what to use and that way we'll both stay in business."

"Yes sir."

I took his advice, and as the season wore on it worked. I still didn't know a doodlebug from a jitterbug, but when my Found passenger showed me his tackle box, I was able to point out a lure that my last group had used effectively on lake trout.

My ultimate test came near the end of June when I met David Hayden-Wyeth. Mr. Hayden-Wyeth was a high-powered executive from England. Because of the Dominion Day holiday, he discovered that he had a free day on his business trip to Toronto. Mr. Hayden-Wyeth was the world's most ardent angler. Through associates, he had arranged with the Airways for a one-day fishing trip. It was my job to pick him up at Toronto Island and fly directly to Wauwaskesh Lodge, but first I had to do his shopping. He needed everything: casual clothes, complete fishing gear and provisions.

I cheated a little. I took Oscar Fleming with me to the Canadian Tire store. Oscar was a native of Paradise, born with fish scales under his fingernails. He helped me pick out the equipment.

Hayden-Whatsit turned out to be a fortyish, gung-ho Englishman who spoke in "by joves" and "good shows." He had never been fishing in North America before, so he pumped me for information the entire flight north while he searched through his new tackle.

I felt relatively safe. I knew Clyde Morrison would lend him anything that I might have missed. Clyde met us at the dock when we landed. He rolled his eyes when he saw my passenger decked out in his Bannister Family Discount apparel: yellow rubber boots and a sweatshirt with the cute bears saying, "Welcome to Paradise."

I made the introductions. "Clyde, this is David Hayden-Wyeth, the one-day customer that Pettigrew called you about."

"Pleased to meet you sir."

"A pleasure, by jove. I am looking forward to this. My pilot friend here kindly selected everything I shall need. Good show, what?"

Clyde looked at me in disbelief. I just smiled.

"Yes, that's great. Let's see what you've got here."

"Good show!"

I didn't wait to see Clyde's reaction to the contents of the tackle box. I returned to Paradise to do flying lessons, having arranged to pick up Hayden-Wyeth later that day and fly him back to Toronto.

I must have passed the test. When I retrieved him in the afternoon he was euphoric, and Clyde didn't chew me out. Hayden-Wyeth had a string of six shiny fish that he loaded into the back of the plane. He couldn't take them to England with him, so with a great gesture of generosity, he gave them to me. I calculated that they had cost him over $100 each.

All the way back to Toronto, he talked excitedly about his "smashing good" day, shouting himself hoarse over the din of the Found. He thanked me for my expert outfitting and said he would remember the trip forever. He even liked the Paradise sweatshirt with the bears on it.

"You have the best life in the world, by jove, flying floatplanes around all those remote lakes. I'll wager you fish every day to your heart's content."

"Sure," I lied.

24/ DIGBY

By the beginning of July, the docks at the Airways were a hive of activity. As well as the air service fleet, a procession of private aircraft often vied for space at our docks. Paradise was a popular refueling stop for pleasure pilots on their way to cottages and resorts. The customers were usually doctor/dentist types who could afford to fly up from Toronto in their own floatplanes.

When we had time between flights, the Airways pilots helped one-speed Sam clear any backlog of airplanes waiting for refueling. It was refreshing to get close to those newer planes with their gleaming factory paint jobs and interiors that didn't smell of dead fish, moose quarters and stale beer.

I was helping Sam on gas the day I witnessed the awkward arrival of a sorry-looking Piper J-3 Cub. It approached from over the town and dove toward the open bay. It never really flared out. With only a slight raising of the nose, its pontoons smacked the water hard, bouncing the airplane through its own spray several times before coming to rest. It sagged lopsided in the water, barely remaining afloat.

I realized I was still holding my breath as the airplane taxied to the dock. It was sad. The J-3 was the original 1930s version of the Supercub, but you wouldn't have known it seeing this airplane. It looked like a kid's toy three years after Christmas. The faded yellow fabric was accented by dark oil streaks running back from the engine. In several places rips were secured by liberal amounts of grey duct tape. One drooping wing was supported by a pair of bent struts and the top of the rudder had been squashed in a previous accident. The fuselage carried the remains of an American registration and the sawed-off wooden propeller was borrowed from a swamp buggy. When it parked among the other visitors, the J-3 looked like a hobo at a church social.

A middle-aged pilot hopped out. He resembled his airplane. His rumpled clothes were topped with a greasy old cap and his lopsided grin was surrounded by a craggy face and a red nose.

"I need some of that avgas, eh?" His friendly tone made the statement a request rather than a demand.

Local floatplane owners rarely stopped at the Airways. They shunned the pricey avgas we sold, preferring instead to burn untaxed boat fuel, snowmobile mix or moonshine. When they did visit our docks it was usually because their airplanes started to wheeze.

"Yes, sir; that stuff otta make 'er right, eh? She's been runnin' poorly this last while," he said.

I didn't know if I was supposed to comment on this fine maintenance decision or not, so I said nothing.

I filled up the J-3's nose tank while he dug out a five-gallon outboard motor tank from the cabin.

"Might as well git the reserve while we're here, eh?"

It was the reserve indeed. I could see the small hole that he had cut in the bottom of the windshield. A garden hose ran through it connecting the airplane's nose tank to the squeeze bulb of the reserve can that he had taken from the baggage compartment. I filled it as well.

"Say, are you the new flying instructor fella?" he asked casually.

"Yes sir," I replied and introduced myself.

"Pleased to meet ya. I'm Digby Olson from up Rum Point way. Folks mostly just call me Dig. I've been meaning to talk to you, eh. I'll have to come back 'ere sometime to see about gittin' my pilot licence. I took some lessons 'ere a while back. The instructor sent me solo after five hours and I thought that was it, eh."

He carefully unfolded an old piece of paper from his wallet and offered it to me. It was a student pilot permit that had expired two years ago.

His confession was still sinking in as he continued. "I bought this 'ere airplane last winter eh, but somebody told me I need more lessons to git a licence."

He edged closer to the J-3 during this last sentence, driven perhaps by my surprised look.

At that time the government minimum for a pilot licence was thirty-five hours of flight training. Most students needed more to reach flight test standards and that was on properly maintained aircraft. I thought he was lucky to be still alive.

I tried to sound casual because he was looking at me sideways. I felt that he would jump into his floating wreck and disappear forever if I pressed him too hard. "That's right, Digby; there are several more lessons after the first solo, including some cross-country work."

My reply was standard enough, but it must have sounded hollow to a guy who had been happily flying his own aircraft after training just five hours.

"Well, I flew this 'ere machine back from Rochester, New York, on skis last winter, by myself," he announced proudly. "I nearly made it all the way, eh. Ran into a snowstorm just south of 'ere and flipped her over on a frozen lake."

One look at the airplane told me Digby wasn't pulling my leg. This guy needed help. He had already demonstrated his lack of training on arrival, and his airplane was obviously unsafe. I didn't want to scare him off by quoting rules and regulations, but he needed more lessons. Of course, the last thing I wanted was to climb into the J-3 with him. Should I chain his plane to the dock and call the sheriff or just forget about it? I felt like a rookie cop sent out on a building ledge to counsel someone contemplating suicide.

"There are still some lessons you should do before taking a flight test."

"A flight test, eh; I didn't know about that. Anything else I gotta do?"

"A written exam."

He didn't like the sound of that. He started inching cautiously toward the airplane again. I decided to try another tack before I lost him altogether.

"Digby, our mechanic could fix your airplane up so it would fly better."

"Oh, she flies great; just runs a mite rough. Didn't you see my landing?" He was smiling, obviously pleased with himself.

I was fighting a losing battle.

"Well, he could stop the wheezing in the motor. You would be surprised what a difference a smooth motor makes. Have you ever had a mechanic do an annual Certificate of Airworthiness inspection on it?"

Somehow I knew the answer.

"The guy I bought 'er from said she was certified, eh."

"Well, there are things to do on an airplane when it is imported."

"Is that so?" Digby replied. I was definitely losing him.

"When you buy an airplane in the United States you must apply for a Canadian Aircraft Registration and Certificate of Airworthiness." I tried to make it sound like scratching a lottery ticket, but he was looking worried. It was too much. I still hadn't mentioned certified repairs to his airplane or federal sales tax owing, and he was making moves to depart.

"Well, thanks for the information, eh. How much do I owe you for the gas?" he asked with a nervous grin.

Digby was an untrained pilot flying an unsafe airplane. The lack of paperwork was secondary. I was in a quandary. One part of me didn't want to get involved. If he wanted to kill himself that was his business. On the other hand, he might take someone with him. It was a tough situation for a young flying instructor.

"$12.58," I replied.

While making his change I took a last lame stab at helping him.

"Would you like to book some flying lessons while you're here?"

"No thanks, I have to run, eh, but I'll give ya a call."

After several hand flips of the short prop, the engine coughed to life, and he was off. The airplane needed a long run across the bay before it staggered into the air, good wing first, and turned north.

In armchair hindsight, it is easy to say I should have done more to set him right. I don't have any defense except that I followed the frailties of human nature and let him go. I could say that I tried to contact him after his visit, but it would be a lie. I thought about him occasionally, but it was a busy summer and I never spoke to him again.

Digby Olson was killed the following February when he flew into a snowfall. The whiteout conditions obliterated his visual references. He lost control of the old Cub and spun into the frozen lake near his house. J-3's spin slowly, and he might have survived the crash if the unsecured gas can had not come forward on impact and taken his head off. He was by himself.

25/ BANNER DAYS

I had heard horror stories about working for bush operators before joining the Airways. I came in spite of them. My desire to fly float planes was stronger than my belief in the stories. The image of bush flying, as perceived by many people in the flying industry, was a modern type of slavery where there were only two ways out: die or get fired. The bush operators were said to make their pilots fly overloaded, poorly maintained airplanes in dangerous weather. If a pilot refused, they always had three others who wanted the job. When I met Bannister, the very look of him declared that all of those things were true.

I took the position anyway. I believed my sense of self-preservation was sound enough that I would quit before flying into an unsafe situation. By July, I had discovered that I was wrong. If I was going to have a problem, it would be my own doing, or undoing. I had already proven that, by flying the damaged Cessna back from the French River and by chasing transport trucks up the Trans Canada Highway in the Supercub. Neither of these stunts had been the result of pressure from the management. My biggest surprise while working at the Airways was finding out that Clifford Bannister, despite his outward appearance of an overgrown blowhard, was really a pussycat—who could fly.

One day I arrived at work in time to see a Supercub taxiing out. I couldn't remember any Cub trips on the booking sheets. Since I was responsible for all the training and rental flights, I hotfooted into the office. There was nothing signed out on the daily flight log.

"Beverly, who's in the Supercub?"

"Mr. Bannister."

"Bannister? I didn't know he had a pilot licence."

Beverly was always afraid of doing something wrong, so she immediately looked worried.

"Beverly, does Mr. Bannister have a pilot licence?"

"I don't know."

I had never seen Bannister fly, but I realized that the answer to my question didn't matter. They were his airplanes. If he wanted to take off in the Cub, there was little I could do to stop him. I certainly wasn't going out in another airplane to chase him down.

These thoughts were running through my head when Jake came in.   "Jake, does Bannister have a pilot licence?" I asked.

"What does he need a pilot licence for?" No one ever got a straight answer from Jake.

"To fly a Supercub. He's taxiing out in LAI right now."

"If he had a pilot licence," he said, while pouring himself a coffee, "Would he fly any better?"

"Jake, has the man ever flown before?"

After taking a sip of his coffee, he said, "Relax, he flew Lancasters in the war."

"Jake, that was a long time ago. That doesn't really qualify him to fly a Supercub."

"He did twenty-eight missions over Germany—without a scratch. He started this air service in 1948 with two Aeronca Chiefs on floats. He and Henry flew night and day."

"Okay, okay, I get the picture," I said. It still didn't make the man current, but I could tell that Jake was going to drag this one on forever.

Before he could continue, Bannister's voice boomed over the radio.

"Beverly! What's the registration of this damn airplane?"

None of our airplanes had their registrations displayed in view of the pilot.

"Here Bev, let me talk to him," Jake said, as he took the microphone out of her hand.

He pushed the button and said in an official voice, "Which airplane would you like to know the registration of, sir?"

"The Supercub, damn it, I'm in the Supercub."

"Well sir, we have two Supercubs. Which Supercub are you in?"

"Who is this? I'm in the Supercub taxiing out. I just want the registration to announce my takeoff."

I realized that Jake was having some fun at Bannister's expense. It didn't seem like a good idea to me, but he was enjoying himself.

"Would you be in the red and yellow Supercub or the yellow and red Supercub?"

There was a short silence. Jake was grinning from ear to ear. I visualized the Supercub in question coming full power up the beach and Bannister charging out and ramming the microphone down Jake's throat.

"Is that Jake? Listen you dumb jerk, when I come back, I'm going to get Noonan to put long range tanks in the Found and I'm going to send you toward Toronto so I never have to see you again."

"The registration is Lima Alpha Yankee."

There was another short silence. Jake was still smiling.

Bannister's voice came back, "L-A-Y, don't you wish! I never bought an airplane registered L A Y, but it will do for now. Lima Alpha Yankee is departing Paradise for a local flight southwest."

An hour later I was walking down to the dock with a student when Bannister returned. He executed a perfect landing as if to emphasize my wasted concern. Sam helped him dock.

When he crawled out, Bannister said, "Sam, get Noonan to post the registration on the instrument panel of the Supercub."

Sam was eager to please his boss. "Which Supercub, Mr. Bannister?"

"Both Supercubs, Sam," he replied with a sigh.

"The registrations are different Mr. Bannister," Sam said nervously.

I thought Bannister might explode.

"Sam, I'll tell Noonan myself."

"Yes sir, Mr. Bannister."

26/ HALF PRICE

July brought Susan and me our first visitors to Paradise. Bob and
Betty Woodfield were friends from our high school days. They
drove up in their MGB and pitched a pup tent in the campsite next
to ours. We were happy to see them, because we were having trouble making friends with people our own age. Most of them had
moved out of town.

It was also our first chance to enjoy the recreational side of living
in Paradise. We both took a day off, and I arranged a boat rental
from Bannister Marina. It was a standing policy that Bannister employees received 50 percent off at all Bannister establishments. That
was an incredibly generous deal considering Bannister owned half
the businesses in town.

I rented the biggest boat available, a 135 horsepower in-
board/outboard runabout. It normally cost $39 a day, plus
lifejackets, plus water skis, plus charts and plus fuel. Barry Torrance
at the marina threw in the charts, jackets and skis for nothing, because I had been extra nice to him when I took his family for a sightseeing flight, at half price. My employee price for the rental would
be $19.50 and the gas. I had set aside $30 for the occasion, about two
days' take-home pay.

The boat was really sharp. It was a brand-new, top-of-the-line
fibreglass model that had yet to see a full season of tourist abuse. It
had two fuel tanks and lots of chrome. The rain held off, so we put
the canvas top down and roared off to explore some of the 30,000 islands of Georgian Bay.

We toured southwest of Paradise which is cottage country for
many rich businessmen and politicians. We felt a part of the scene as
we cruised past their expensive summer homes in our flashy boat. It
seemed a world away from living in a tent.

We pulled up to a small uninhabited rock island and used it as a
base for a picnic and some water skiing. Bob went first. I hit full
power and the boat jerked him off the rock so fast that he didn't get
wet. The inboard/outboard pulled him along at fifty kilometres per
hour! We took turns roaring around most of the afternoon. By the

time we quit, we had used up one tank of gas and a good part of the other.

The four of us cruised back to the marina, sunburned and happy. It had been a good day. Barry refueled the boat while we unloaded our picnic gear. It seemed to take him a long time.

"You folks must have had a lot of fun. You used eighty-five gallons."

My mouth went dry. "Eighty-five gallons! Barry, you must be kidding. How much does it hold?"

"About one hundred gallons, 50 each side. The fuel comes to $45.58, but you get 50 percent off, so that makes it $22.79 plus $19.50 for the rental."

I only had $30. "Gee Barry, could I charge that until pay day?" I was very embarrassed.

"I can't apply your discount if you do. Then you would owe over $80."

Bob came over and helped me out. He chipped in the $10 that he had saved to take us all out to dinner. With that and Susan's change, I paid the bill.

That evening we sat around the campfire, eating macaroni and cheese. It started to rain. When we were huddled in the tent, dog and all, Bob said, "Now I've seen how both halves live."

27/ DANNY

By July, I was teaching six students on the Private Pilot Course. I found it easier instructing on float planes. The Paradise locals had all grown up in boats, so their water handling was no problem. Teaching them to take off and land on floats in the wide open bay was not as difficult as getting the big-city students to control those dinky tires on the narrow strips of asphalt. The fact that I was using Supercubs helped too. The airplane had the horsepower to pull students out of messed-up approaches, yet it flew at slow-motion speeds compared to other flight trainers. All my students were completing the course near the thirty-five hour minimum, and I found that I was actually enjoying instructing again.

So I didn't mind when a new student came into the Airways. Danny Schribner was a lean, good-looking twenty-year-old with bright blue eyes set in a deeply tanned face. Danny told me that he wanted to learn how to fly. There was one big problem. He was disabled.

Danny had suffered the same fate as too many Paradise teenagers. When he was in high school, he went on a drunken joy ride with some friends. They missed one of the Trans Canada curves that cut through Precambrian rock.

Ken Noonan was the ambulance driver that night and he remembered the scene. "There were no skid marks; they just plain missed the curve. The car went straight into the rock face at high speed. The three kids in the front were hamburger, killed instantly. Danny was one of two guys in the back who survived."

The accident left Danny with both ankles fused and limited use of his knees, but it also gave him a new respect for life. The incredible fact that he could walk at all was an indication of his determination. He used a cane and swung his legs from his hips. When he finished high school, Danny got a job operating a backhoe. He saved up enough money to learn to fly and came to the Airways.

I never liked to see anyone waste their money on flying lessons. If there was no hope of their getting a pilot licence, I tried to take a hard line with them right off. I felt it was better to disappoint these

91

people early, rather than drag it out until their money was all gone, even if it meant that I had to be the bad guy to break the news.

I looked straight into Danny's resolute face, saw his intense blue eyes and said, "Well Danny, first you need a pilot medical. Make an appointment with Doctor Spooner at the medical centre and he'll see if you're fit to fly. Then come back and see me."

It was true; all pilots needed a standard medical before receiving their student pilot permit. Dr. Spooner was the local M.D. designated by the Department of Transport to give these examinations. I knew that I was passing the bad news buck to Spooner, but I rationalized that, as a doctor, he would be more familiar with disappointing people. Danny could have started flying lessons without a medical. The permit was not needed until he was ready to fly solo, but I didn't tell him that, because I knew he would be wasting his money.

I thought I had seen the last of Danny Schribner. It was too bad. He seemed like a nice kid. I had just about forgotten him when he came back two weeks later with a letter in his hand and a big smile on his face. He had passed the pilot medical with flying colours. His weight, vision, hearing, blood pressure, lungs and muscle tone were all specimen perfect. Of course they were, the kid could do one-armed chin ups, all day, while reading a book! But he could hardly walk. Surely the doctor had noticed that.

He had. The letter was from the Department of Transport. Because Danny's medical report noted, "reduced motor skills in the lower appendages due to a previous accident", they requested that he be tested by a pilot standards inspector prior to receiving his student pilot permit.

That meant that Danny would have to learn to fly before being tested to see if he had the mobility to learn to fly. I would have to recommend him for the test.

I looked at him and said, "The inspector may come and say no."

The intensity was still there. It always was. "He won't; you'll see. When can we start?"

We started right away. He was amazing. When we went flying, he tossed his cane into the back and hauled himself around the pre-flight inspection with his powerful arms. When he needed both hands for something like pumping out the floats, he just sat down. He had the annoying habit of making me feel that my own faculties, although complete, were not fully developed. In the cockpit, he worked the rudder pedals by swinging his hips in the seat. He had a beautiful touch on the control stick. The backhoe work had fine-tuned his hand/eye control and his boating experience took care of the rest. He listened intently when I spoke and between lessons he studied the textbooks. After six flights, he was probably ready to go solo.

The inspector was scheduled for ten days after Danny had started his flying. The man drove up from Toronto. At stake was Danny's money and his future as a pilot, but I was the one who was nervous. I felt like we were about to meet God.

Danny sat relaxing in the office. "Why are you pacing?" he asked.

"I'm nervous; you should be pacing too," I replied, without thinking.

"I can't pace; besides, I'm not nervous. Everything is going to be fine, relax."

It was a clear day but windy. The inspector arrived at ten o'clock. He wasn't God. He was Inspector Kennedy from my own instructor flight test earlier in the summer. He stood in our office stone-faced and still dressed like an undertaker.

After meeting Danny, Kennedy looked out across the bay at the waves. They were being driven by gusts up to twenty knots. He said to me, "Would you fly with a student in this wind?"

When I thought about it afterward, I realized that his tone was searching for a no, but I answered without reflection.

"Yes sir," I replied.

He frowned and said, "Would you send a student solo in a strong wind like this?"

Now I was thinking. This guy had the power to do more than deny Danny a permit. His department monitored all the flying schools and instructors. Maybe he was testing me.

"Well, that would depend; certainly not a first solo." I watched him to see if this was the right answer.

"Right. Then it wouldn't be fair to Danny here, to expect him to demonstrate his ability to fly the airplane in weather conditions unsuitable for first solo, now would it?" His look was demanding a no.

"No sir," I replied.

I think Danny would have said something different, but out of respect for us he said nothing. Inspector Kennedy suggested that we call his office and book another test. Why the man drove three hours to ask me about the wind, I have no idea. I think he didn't like me after Buttonville Tower chewed him out for my lack of navigation skill. Whatever, he left.

I was disappointed. I never liked wasting nervousness. Danny was irrepressible. He said, "Come on hotshot; at least he didn't say no to the permit. Make that phone call, and then let's go flying. You can show me why I wouldn't go first solo in this wind."

It was a week before the next appointment. Danny and I flew several more lessons and he was doing well. The scene on the day of the test was the same. Danny relaxed in a chair while I paced. At least it wasn't windy.

A different inspector came through the door. He didn't look like God or an undertaker, but somewhere in between. Inspector Donaldson had a friendly air about him that raised my spirits. After we were all introduced, he pulled up a chair opposite Danny and stuck his feet out.

"Dan, I want you to pretend that my feet are the rudder pedals. Push on them as hard as you can, one at a time."

Danny obliged, twisting in his chair, first left and then right, hard enough to move the inspector backward.

"That's good," Donaldson smiled, "now let's go down to the airplane."

He followed Danny out the door, watching him negotiate the stairs and the slope to the dock. So did I.

"Okay Dan, I would like to see you climb into the plane."

Danny hung his cane on the strut, grabbed the windshield brace and swung himself into the pilot seat in one smooth motion.

"Move the rudder pedals, please," Donaldson asked.

The rudder banged as he moved them right to the stops.

"Fine. Now climb out."

Danny grabbed the windshield brace and in a swish and a plop, he was on the dock, retrieving his cane. Without saying anything, Donaldson kicked the cane out from under him. Danny stood there like a rock.

"What do you need the cane for?" the inspector asked.

"Walking. When I put my right leg forward, the knee won't lock and when my weight is on it, it bends."

"You seem to get around all right."

"Yes sir, I do; thank you."

"One more question. How would you paddle the Supercub, if it was necessary?

"I sit down on the float with my legs in the water. Would you like me to show you?"

"No, that isn't necessary."

I summoned an optimistic voice and asked, "Would you like to go flying now?"

"No thank you; I think I've seen enough."

Oh, no! I thought.

Donaldson smiled and said, "You and Dan might want to go flying. I think we have held up his progress long enough. Come back into the office, and I'll give Dan a temporary student permit. He can use it until he gets one in the mail. This man is going to be a pilot."

It was the expression on Dan's face that I remember most from that moment. It was a happy expression, of course, but it wasn't a look of humble joy. The smile on his face said, "You can bet on that one, Mister."

Donaldson explained that there would be some restrictions. Danny could fly any airplane on floats or skis, but his wheel endorsement, if he chose to get one, would only be valid for aircraft with a hand brake and no toe or heel brakes. Paradise had no airport for landplanes at the time, so the restrictions presented no hardships for Danny.

I sent him on his first solo that same afternoon. There was no reason not to. When he returned I took advantage of his handicap by jerking him into the bay before he grabbed his cane.

He swam back to the dock smiling and said, "Could you give a cripple a hand?"

"No way Danny. I've worked here long enough to recognize that trick."

"Well then, at least hand me my cane."

I did, and he used it to hook me into the lake.

28/ BOTTOMS UP

The last trip on Fridays during the summer was usually the Miss Bottomsworth Supercub flight. Miss Penelope Bottomsworth was the headmistress of a private school for girls. She was a pompous, never-married lady in her fifties who always wore her grey hair so severely pulled back that she had to purse her lips to keep her mouth closed. She had an apple-doll face and a sour disposition. Jake called her "Bottoms Up", when she wasn't around. In her presence it was always "Miss Bottomsworth."

She would arrive at the Airways every Friday with a carpetbag and Fluffy, her white French Poodle. One of us would fly her to her cottage for a weekend of solitude. She was so miserable that we always drew straws to see who would do it.

Jake pulled the short straw on the Friday before a day off. He had planned a dinner date that evening with his girlfriend in Barrie, one hundred kilometres to the south. He pleaded with us, but nothing in the world would entice Len or me to switch with him.

He saved time by going home and changing before the flight. When Miss Bottomsworth arrived, Jake was standing by the plane dressed in his best clothes including a tie, pressed pants and leather shoes.

Miss Bottomsworth didn't acknowledge his attire, but that was typical since she only spoke to complain. She often called us "louts" if we didn't rush to help with her bag, or she would scold us for not being ready at the precise time she had booked the airplane. To her we were "common rabble", to be tolerated only because of the time saved by flying.

Jake was ready this time. He took off with Miss Bottomsworth sitting silently in the back seat with Fluffy on her lap. The trouble started on arrival at the cottage. The Supercub had just one door and it was on the right side. That evening, a steady breeze dictated docking into the wind which would put the dock on the left side.

To accomplish this, Jake would have to charge the dock and shut down the engine well back. As the Cub lost momentum, he would have to climb out onto the right float, slide under the engine on the spreader bar (without touching the hot exhaust pipe), hop onto the dock from the left float, grab the airplane and turn it around. It was a difficult enough manoeuvre dressed in jeans and sneakers. Jake told us about it when he came in to work on the following Sunday.

"On the first try, I misjudged the wind strength and took too long getting across. When I reached for the dock, we were already drifting backwards out of reach. There was nothing I could do except crawl back to the other side and into the airplane to start over again. For the second try, I managed to speed things up without wrecking my clothes, but I was almost too late. We were beginning to drift away. I jumped the gap onto the dock, but when I turned to catch the plane, she was gone.

"There I was, standing on the dock in my good duds on a Friday night, watching Bottoms Up and Fluffy drift toward the rocks in the Supercub. I did the only thing I could; I stripped. There was no way I was going to ruin my good clothes. I took everything off down to my boxers and dove in after her.

"At first, I thought she was screaming because she was drifting helplessly away. When I got closer, I could hear that she was yelling, 'Get away from me you brute; don't you touch me.'

"Whatever gave the old bag the idea I wanted to touch her? I was just trying to save the airplane from the rocks. Maybe she was playing hard-to-get. Anyway, I reached the plane and climbed onto the float. I tried to ignore her, but she started to hit me with her purse. I've got bruises on my shoulders. The dog joined in the act, yapping his stupid little head off.

"I fired up the airplane and headed for the dock again, with her still screaming and the mutt barking. This time I made a quick exit, but I was so flustered that I slipped on the spreader bar. I burned my back on the exhaust pipe, but I did catch the dock. While I held the airplane for her, in my dripping drawers, the thankless old bat yelled at me to stay away from her. She grabbed her bag and the mutt and bustled up to the cottage where she slammed the door.

"I gathered up my clothes and happened to look back. The sly old fox was watching me through a window. I waved, but she closed the curtain. I put my clothes on the passenger seat and flew back with the window open to dry off."

When Len and I had stopped laughing, I said, "Someone has to bring her out this evening. I don't think any of us can top your performance Jake, you should be the one to get her."

"No way. If it's my trip, she stays there 'til Christmas," he said and then walked away.

Len and I flipped for it, and I lost. That evening I arrived at her cottage on time. When she spoke, it was brief, but I found it very interesting.

"Where is the pilot who brought me here?"

"He is on another flight; we take turns doing different ones."

"I would like him to be my pilot next week."

"Yes, Miss Bottomsworth," I answered.

29/ DUDLEY AND THE MAD DOG

Monday was Odd Couple day at the Airways. The Odd Couple was Dudley Crane and Mad Dog McClintock, two men who were land use specialists from the Ministry of Soil and Sea. It was their job to spend a week on government land and study its use. Each Monday, Henry would fly them to a different lake in the district where they would camp for the week and observe. Their mandate was to record what they saw during their stay. They noted the birds and the bees, the flowers and the trees, the fish they caught and wildlife they saw. Their destinations were usually remote lakes, only accessible by airplane. If it was raining, threatening to rain or forecast to rain on Monday, Dudley and Mad Dog wouldn't go. They went on Tuesday instead, if it wasn't raining.

They would arrive at the Airways in their Soil and Sea truck with a mountain of gear that would choke the Beaver. They had a four-burner camping stove, an eight-man tent, cots, five days' food, clothing and beer, pots and pans, water purifier, fishing gear, a two-way radio, life jackets, paddles, motor, gas and anything else that would ease the strain of spending five days in the bush. It was all piled into the plane, except the square-back canoe which Henry tied onto the left float.

I met the Odd Couple on the Airways dock one Monday when they were helping Henry load for a trip into the bush. They were as different as any two men could be. Dudley Crane was the original kick-sand-in-his-face weakling. His thinning hair and wire-rim glasses made him look like he would be more at home in a bank than struggling to load the heavy boxes into the Beaver.

"Mad Dog" was McClintock's nickname, but no one called him anything else. If his mother had named him Sue, none of us wanted to be the first to ask. As the name Mad Dog implied, he was the opposite to Dudley. He was a head over two metres tall and built like a locomotive. When he stepped onto one of the Beaver's floats carrying a box under each massive arm, the two-ton airplane bobbed in the water like a canoe. When he spoke, his deep voice sounded like it was coming from the bottom of his size fourteen boots. Despite their obvious physical differences, the two men seemed to work cheerfully together.

"Here you go, Henry," Dudley Crane said, "this is a light one, but mind you don't squish Teddy in there."

Mad Dog added good naturedly, "Yes Henry, mind Teddy. I have to live with Dudley all week, and it would be unbearable if you suffocated his little fur-faced friend."

Dudley countered the friendly jab with, "This is a heavy one, Henry. Don't jostle it. It contains Mad Dog's radio, and there would be hell to pay if he missed a night of Stompin' Tom Conners."

It occurred to me that these two guys had a cushy job. They spent five days in the bush at the government's expense and their most strenuous activity was fishing.

I got to know them a little better when Henry wasn't able to bring them out on a Friday. The weather was rainy, and we didn't turn a propellor all day. Saturday began foggy, but the forecast called for clearing. Our charter schedule was well backed up. It was decided that I would pick up Dudley and Mad Dog in the Found, leaving most of their gear until Henry was free with the Beaver.

As soon as the fog started to lift, I took off for their lake. It wasn't an easy flight because lingering shreds of cloud clung to the hilltops along the way. I made it by staying down and weaving in and out of the valleys.

When I landed, I could see the two men waiting on the rocky shore. They were one hundred metres apart, each sitting on a separate pile of gear. I didn't know which one to head for first, so I aimed in between them and shut down. When I opened my door, they both started yelling at once.

"Where have you been?"

"Why didn't you come on Thursday before the weather turned bad?"

"Shut up Dudley; I'm talking to him. Hey boy, where's Henry?"

"You shut up Mad Dog; I'm in charge here. Where's the Beaver? We can't all go in that thing."

"Load me first."

"No, I'm in charge; load me first."

I guided the drifting Found to a flat rock halfway between them. They rushed the plane. I stepped ashore and held the wing until I realized that I was going to be in the middle of a collision. I moved back just in time. Mad Dog reached the Found first with his giant thundering strides, but as he folded himself to fit under the wing, Dudley scooted onto the float in front of him. Mad Dog picked him up and dropped him back onto shore. Then he climbed into the back seat of the airplane. Dudley yelled and cursed as he picked himself up and scrambled into the front seat.

With Mad Dog in the back, the Found sat with her nose stuck in the air and the water rudders buried under the surface. I hated to stir them up even more, but weighted down in the rear, the reluctant Found would never make it onto the step during the takeoff.

I stuck my head in the cockpit and said as soothingly as possible, "Excuse me, gentlemen; you'll have to switch seats to balance the airplane."

"He always rides up front," Dudley whined, "I'm in charge, I should sit here."

"Dudley, you dumb jerk," Mad Dog's voice boomed, "he can't fly the plane with little runts in the front."

"Oh yeah, if I'm so dumb, how come you climbed into the back?"

"Because you got in my way."

"Gentlemen!" I had to yell to be heard over their arguing, "Unless you want to stay here, stop fighting and switch seats."

They both moved at once. Dudley dove for the back just as Mad Dog was moving forward. There was a loud crack as they banged heads. It was just what they needed. Neither man was hurt badly and the bashing took the starch out of their arguing.

Mad Dog realized that he couldn't fit between the seats to move up front so he stepped out of the airplane onto the float. Dudley slid into the back. The only thing that kept the Found from sinking tail first was the fact that the floats were already resting on the bottom in the shallow water.

I climbed into the front after Mad Dog. His shoulders were so big that I couldn't close my door. He sat there rubbing his head and looking out the window. I didn't want to rile him by asking for more room; besides, he probably didn't have any. I turned sideways with my back to my door and flew the airplane home from there. I used my right hand on the control wheel and crossed my left hand over to work the throttle. With my right leg tucked under me, I used my left leg for both rudder pedals. It was awkward, but the worst part was that I was looking right at Mad Dog. I hoped that we would make it to Paradise before he thought I was staring at him on purpose.

It was Sunday afternoon before Henry and I were in the office at the same time. I told him about the trip. "When I picked up your friends Dudley and Mad Dog yesterday, they were like a couple of lunatics."

"They're like that at the end of every week; like two wolves on a bone, especially if I'm late. I wouldn't be surprised to find them both axed to death some rainy Friday, but they always come back the next week as friendly as muskrats in heat."

30/ MEDIVAC

The Monday afternoon flight southbound was rough. A broken layer of low cloud had forced me to fly in the turbulence near the ground. The customer beside me in the Found looked green and unhappy, but he wasn't nearly as uncomfortable as his friend in the rear seat. My two passengers were Americans from Detroit who had been on a little fishing jaunt to Paradise. The guy lying in the back was a kidney failure patient who was using his three days between stints on a dialysis machine for a little holiday. It had been a mistake.

A few beers against doctor's orders had turned a fun weekend into agony. The poisons building in his body were slowly killing him. Arrangements had been made for an ambulance to meet us at the Toronto Island float base. As we flew over the city centre, I contacted the Island Control Tower which handled the air traffic in that area.

"Island Tower, this is Found, Sierra Bravo Delta on floats from Paradise. I'm approaching your zone for landing in the harbour."

"Sierra Bravo Delta, Island Tower, the wind is from 090 degrees at 30 knots, gusting to 35, altimeter 29.42. Be advised there is rough water in the harbour with waves reported over a metre. A Cessna One-Eighty-Five on floats did a low pass here thirty minutes ago and elected to return north rather than land."

Darn. The wind direction gave the strong gusts the full length of the harbour to stir up rough water. Usually the prevailing winds were southwest and the islands protected the landing area. The only problem that I had ever encountered at Toronto was finding room to land among the packs of summertime pleasure craft. There were no boats now. As we drew closer to the shore, I could see the normally placid bay was a cauldron of murky whitecaps.

It had been a bad day. A frantic radiotelephone call from a remote fishing camp had interrupted our full flying schedule. Jake had brought the kidney patient out of the bush to the Paradise hospital, delaying some of our other trips, but without a dialysis machine they could do nothing for him. Several phone calls later it had been determined there was no extra dialysis time available in Toronto. Finally his own doctor had made arrangements for him in Detroit. He had to get there as soon as possible.

The front seat passenger heard my exchange with the control tower over the cabin speaker. He waited anxiously for my reply. There was no way even the good old Yellow Submarine could withstand a landing in those waves without damage. The nearest sheltered water was Lake Wilcox, thirty kilometres north where no ambulance was waiting. Another look at the boiling harbour gave me an idea.

"No problem," I assured the fellow beside me. He smiled nervously and reached over and stuffed a five-dollar American bill into my shirt pocket.

The five dollars didn't influence me to take unnecessary risks. I wouldn't have gambled three lives to save one, but I didn't refuse the money either. Not on your life. The tip didn't affect my decision to land, but it made it more fun.

"Island Tower, Sierra Bravo Delta; is our ambulance at the dock?"

"Roger SBD, ambulance standing by, but the wind just hit forty knots. Do you intend to land or would you like a low pass first?"

"SBD will be landing, Tower."

"Roger, call on a left base by the western gap."

Another five dollars went into my pocket.

The controller could not forbid me to land. It was his job to advise me of wind and traffic, but he knew a landing in those conditions would be foolish. He was pushing hard for me to abort my arrival. What he didn't know was how I was going to modify my approach to survive the rough water.

"SBD is on left base."

"SBD roger, we just had a wind gust hit forty-three knots on the metre, do you still intend to land?"

"Affirmative."

"Land at your own discretion."

I had my hands full flying the airplane. As we descended, the turbulence increased with the high winds deflecting off the waterfront buildings. Five more dollars went into my pocket.

The western entrance to Toronto harbour was a long, cement-walled gap of water only one hundred metres wide. On most summer days it was choked with a tangle of pleasure craft and commercial freighters coming and going from the lake. For good reason it was strictly off limits to floatplanes.

On this blustery day there was no traffic in the gap and best of all, its surface was smooth; the piers were blocking the waves. The ferry that crossed the channel to the airport every fifteen minutes was docked on the island side waiting for the ambulance that was going to transfer my patient to a flight out of Toronto's International

Airport.

I lined up on the thin strip of calm water and reduced the power. The Found dropped between the walls, settled on the glassy surface and glided to a smooth stop. So far, so good. We still had to taxi around the corner through the churning harbour to the floatplane dock, but I knew the Found could handle it at low speed.

Our landing was hidden from the control tower's view by a large hangar. The controller called. He sounded like an accusing high school vice-principal, "Sierra Bravo Delta, Island Tower; did you land in the Western Gap?"

I could have lied and pleaded ignorance, but instead I took the coward's way out; I shut the radio off and taxied into the first of the metre-high rollers. It was rough. The Found struggled up one side of each wave and teetered on the crest before sliding down the other. It crashed into the troughs in a wall of spray thrown up by the prop. I assured the man next to me that everything would be fine and asked him to be ready for a quick exit when we reached the dock. He thanked me for my help and stuffed twenty dollars into my shirt.

Because floatplanes act like large weather vanes in a strong wind, I couldn't turn at our slow speed. I had to taxi past the dock until we were upwind and then shut down the engine to drift backwards. The rough water was tossing the floating dock like a cork. I could see that this was going to be the hardest part of the trip, but there were three airport linecrew riding on the pitching dock, ready to give us a hand. As we approached, a large wave lifted the Found high and dropped us into their laps. We landed with one float on the bouncing dock and the other still in the lake. The surprised linemen somehow managed to stay clear of the charging airplane and recovered to grab the wing, holding us in place.

I stood on the float, reached into the back seat and rudely jerked the patient clean out of the airplane onto the dock. One of the helpers pulled him out of the way. The Found shifted restlessly with each wave and I knew the dock hands couldn't hold on long. The guy in the front was still fumbling with their hand luggage so I grabbed and yanked him out, bags and all.

Starving pilots never tip starving linecrew, but this time I yelled, "Beers on me," over the roar of the wind and stuffed one of the five-dollar bills into the nearest shirt. I jumped into the pilot seat as the very next wave tilted the dock and slid the airplane into the drink. Thankfully the Found always started on the first try; I was dangerously close to the sea wall.

Lightly loaded and facing into the gale, I decided to depart from the dock. With forty knots already blowing over the wings, I only needed to accelerate another twenty to take off. With full power the airplane lifted off the crest of the second wave.

In the rush I had neglected to turn on the radio for departure instructions. If I was in trouble for the landing, I was in big trouble now. I didn't want to hear about it, so I left the radio off and turned north, watching for other air traffic.

The next day dawned clear and calm. Jake flew a regular charter to Toronto Island. By coincidence, he took the Found. When he returned, he burst excitedly into the office and headed straight to where I was filling in log books.

"What did you do when you were at Toronto Island yesterday? When the control tower heard the Found's call sign, they got real hostile. Then when I got to the dock, there were six linecrew waiting. They were so friendly, I thought they were going to kiss me!"

31/ HERE KITTY KITTY

Jake, Len and I were drinking coffee in the pilot shack when Gary walked in and announced that Clifford Bannister was going to hold a staff barbecue at his cottage. It was for all Bannister employees, the over one hundred people who worked in the various parts of his miniature empire.

Gary made it sound like a gesture of goodwill toward the peasants. "I've managed to get you guys invited to a barbecue on Bannister's island a week this Saturday."

"Airways employees are always invited to that party," Jake said.

"They were until you got roaring drunk last year and tried to relieve yourself on Mrs. Bannister's pet cat," Gary replied.

"Oh, I forgot about that," Jake said with a smile and a shrug. "How could I know that Mrs. Bannister was watching?"

"Everyone was watching after you fell into her prize rose bushes," Gary exclaimed.

"I couldn't help it. You try watering a running cat, it's hard to do."

"Lucky for everyone here, Henry is being presented with a gold watch for his twenty-five years with the Airways. I'm helping with the arrangements and I talked Bannister into letting you all come. Jake, you're under strict orders to stay sober and stay away from Mrs. Bannister's cat and her garden."

"Yes sir, General," Jake said, giving him a mock salute, "I'll be a model Airways employee, you'll see."

"Just behave yourself," Gary said, getting in the last word.

The barbecue was a main event in Paradise. It had become an annual mid-summer's break for the townspeople. The ones who didn't work for Bannister were usually married to someone who did. Every business closed early on the big day, leaving the tourists to fend for themselves. Susan and I had been looking forward to the party. To us it was a chance to relax and enjoy our Paradise friends and perhaps meet new ones.

We both worked until closing that afternoon, so we were among the last guests to catch the free transportation to the island in the

Bannister Water Taxi. The old wooden launch was typical of the many water taxis that had served Georgian Bay's cottagers for generations. It had a hard top, was open on all sides, and held about forty people if they all stood up.

Susan was a little nervous around water. She could swim, but she didn't like the idea of swimming to save her life. The look of the old boat bothered her. It had hauled everything to island cottages in the area. People, groceries, plywood, appliances, they had all left their marks on the aging wood, adding to the boat's overused appearance.

"Are you sure this is safe?" Susan asked me as we climbed on board.

The water taxi driver overheard her. "Ma'am, I've bin drivin' this ol' girl fer nye on eighteen y'ars and my pa drove 'er a'for me. I t'ink she be good fer one more trip."

"I hope so," Susan said, smiling nervously.

When we were seated near the stern, she whispered, "I'd feel better if Captain Bligh there had said 'good fer two more trips.' We have to come back in this relic."

Bannister's island was nestled in the middle of the more exclusive vacation real estate, twelve kilometres southwest of Paradise. To get there, the driver threaded his boat carefully through a maze of rocky narrow channels that separated the hundreds of small islands in this area. The dangers of navigating those waters kept the common boaters out, affording privacy to the owners.

Susan relaxed when we were on dry land again. Like the neighbouring cottages, Bannister's place looked more like a house. It was marked off limits for the party. Two marquees were set up on the lawn, one with food and a busier one with free drinks. The party was in full swing when we got there.

"I need a glass of wine to steady my nerves," Susan said.

I led her toward the liquor tent. We saw Jake Lewis coming out with fresh suds slopping from two large plastic cups.

"I see you're flying with both hands tonight Jake," I said.

"You can bet your own mother on that one my son. It's only once a year that the old blowhard loosens his wallet like this. Here's to his health; may he live a thousand years and buy a thousand beers." Jake ended by taking a big swig from one of the cups.

"What about Pettigrew's strict orders?" I asked, just to egg him on.

"Screw Pettigrew," he said, emitting a waft of beer fumes, "but you have reminded me that the only good cat is a wet one."

Jake was already too far gone to worry about anything. He smiled and wandered off, whispering loudly, "Here kitty, kitty. Here kitty, kitty."

Bannister had invited a few of his high-class neighbours to mix with the common folk. Ian Westley was there. When he saw Susan and me sitting down at the tables outside the tents, he came over.

Ian fit the image of a rich, retired race driver: navy blazer, polo shirt, casual slacks, blond hair, blue eyes and Hollywood smile. I made the introductions, "Susan, this is Ian Westley."

"Yes, I remember; you're the racer," she said.

"I'm pleased to meet you," Ian said. "I didn't realize that this guy was harbouring such a beautiful girl up on Grove Lake Hill."

Susan was immune to patronizing greetings from her fashion days, but Ian always sounded genuine. She returned his smile.

"You must talk your husband into bringing you out to our summer house sometime," Ian continued.

I was sure that he was only making automatic small talk, but he was speaking to a girl who had lived in a tent for two months.

Susan said, "When?"

The ready reply didn't seem to bother him. He continued, "Do you play tennis, Susan?"

"No, but I'd love to try," she said quickly.

"Well that settles it then. Come for a tennis lesson. I'll arrange a time around a flying lesson with your husband."

"Fine, thank you," Susan replied.

"You two enjoy the party, and I'll look forward to seeing you soon." He took his leave to circulate among the other guests.

I was a little jealous of Ian's charm, but the thought that flashed through my head at the time made me smile. Susan was my height and weighed a fit seventy-seven kilograms. But in her case, big and strong did not translate into coordinated. Her nickname from high school was "Smash." I had a mental image of Georgian Bay filled with Ian's tennis balls, as Susan belted each one of his serves off the Westley's island.

"He is very nice," she said after he had left.

"Yes he is. Say Smash, since when have you become Billy Jean King?"

"I wasn't going to pass up an invitation to the Westley's just because I haven't played tennis. Maybe he'll invite us for one of those lunches you talk about."

"Are you going to buy a little white tutu for the occasion?" I teased.

"No," she blushed, "can't I go in my jeans?"

"Only if you wash the horse out of them first. But you should buy your own tennis balls."

"Why? Won't they have lots?"

"Yes, but after you're done they won't. Come on, let's get some food."

We lined up for hotdogs and then joined TV cableman Oscar Fleming at a table. Susan had met him before.

"Been fishing lately?" he asked with a chuckle. Oscar knew how much I loved fishing.

I owed him a few wisecracks, so I tried to even the score. "No, but I'd like to watch TV. Do we get 50 percent off if you rig cable to our campsite?"

"No," he smiled, "We don't do tentcalls to hilltop campsites without electricity for people who don't own a TV. Are you looking for pointers in the *Sky King* reruns?"

"Thanks pal. Think twice before you climb a pole when I'm in an airplane."

The highlight of the evening was Bannister's gold watch presentation to Henry. The big boss enjoyed playing patriarch to his gathered employees. He gave a little speech, standing with his arm around Henry.

"Twenty-five years ago, a tall, skinny farm boy with a new pilot licence arrived here from Southern Ontario. He asked me for a flying job. I happened to need a pilot at the time. I had two airplanes, but I was trying to do all the flying myself. The trouble was I didn't know how long I could afford to pay him, so I struck a deal. I said that I would try him out, but if I didn't like the way he worked, I'd have to let him go.

"Well, he flew the floats off those airplanes all summer, and by the end of the year I had made some money for the first time in the history of the Airways. He asked me how he was doing. I didn't know if I could pay him all winter, so I said that I wasn't sure yet, but he could stay on and I'd see how he made out on skis.

"He flew the skis off the airplanes through the winter, and I made more money. Then I decided that this guy probably worked better when he was under the gun, so when he asked me how he was doing again, I told him that I still wasn't sure yet, but he could stay and we would see.

"Well, it's been twenty-five years, Henry, and I'm still not sure how you are going to work out, but I hope you will stay on a little longer."

The crowd roared their approval. Henry was choked up over being the centre of attention. It was the first time that I had seen him at a loss for words. He just shook Bannister's hand and said, "Thanks." There were tears in his eyes. The crowd roared again. Everyone was getting tight, and I think they would have roared at anything.

As darkness fell, Susan and I headed for the water taxi. Being tent people, we usually went to bed when the sun set. It saved lantern fuel.

When we passed Mrs. Bannister's prize rose bushes, I could hear snoring. In the dim light I saw that Jake had fallen into the garden and was sleeping where he had dropped. The best part of the scene was the cat licking the beer from the cup still in Jake's hand.

I knew Jake would be in trouble if Bannister or Pettigrew discovered him, so Susan and I dragged him out of the roses, thorns and all. We managed to wake him up enough so he could help us help him over to a chair by the tents. Len saw us.

"Free beer will do it every time," he said knowingly.

"Yeah, Captain Suds flies again. Susan and I were on our way to the dock when we found him sleeping in the bushes."

"Look, you have tomorrow's first flight. Why don't you two catch the first water taxi home and I'll take care of Jake."

"You sure?" It was an offer we both wanted to accept.

Jake was slumped over and mumbling in his sleep, "Here kitty, kitty."

"Sure. I'll pour some coffee in him and come later."

"Thanks, Len. We appreciate it."

While Susan and I walked back to the dock, I couldn't help feeling good about working for Bannister. He didn't have to spring for the party, but he did. A gold watch for Henry, free food, booze, and a boat ride for everyone; it was a nice gesture.

32/ WATER PILOT

When Susan and I reached Bannister's dock there were a few other couples waiting on board the water taxi, but no driver. Someone went looking for him and found the man passed out under a tree. They threw some water on him and brought him to the boat.

It was his party as much as anyone else's, but when Susan saw this guy being helped into his seat, she went rigid as a cat being carried to bath water. I didn't think Bannister was going to invite two hundred of us to stay for the night, so I coaxed her on board.

"It will be all right. These water taxi drivers usually drink and drive." It was true. They had dashboard holders for their beer bottles. She was still scared.

Our driver started the boat, put it into gear and drove straight across the narrow channel onto the rocks on the other shore. The boat lurched to a stop with its propellor still churning and the driver slumped over the wheel. No one was hurt, because the boat had not been travelling very fast when it hit. The impact unleashed a scream from Susan followed by her best I-told-you-so look.

Someone threw us a line from Bannister's dock and pulled us back. The boat now became the centre of attention. Most of the party-goers were milling around the dock. Susan and I jumped ashore. Several self-styled experts began looking for damage in the bilge, using matches and lighters. Apparently there were no bad leaks and no fumes either. They pronounced everything fit, except the driver.

"I'm not getting back on that boat," Susan said in a steady voice.

I understood how she felt, but I wasn't looking forward to telling Bannister that we needed to use his food tent for the night because my wife was afraid to ride the water taxi in the dark. We sat down in silence.

A few minutes later someone said that they had found another driver and were set to shove off. I looked at Susan.

"I'll make you a deal," she said. "If the taxi comes back from the first load in one piece, then the new driver must be okay and we could go with the next group."

"Okay," I replied.

"But we have to ride in the back of the boat or I don't go," she added.

"Fine," I said.

"And we have to wear life jackets."

Macho bush pilots didn't wear life jackets, but it still beat staying overnight. "Okay, it's a deal. Anything else?"

"Yes. I need a glass of wine." That was my girl.

The taxi returned in an hour and three glasses of wine later. We lined up at the dock and when it was our turn to board we edged our way to the stern. It was standing room only, but I managed to pull two life jackets from the roof storage nets. They were the old lumpy square ones, held together by doubtful-looking straps. They were dusty and moldy, but no mice fell out when I took them down. The people around us stared as we fought to get them on in our limited space. I really didn't care at that point.

The launch was jammed full. We couldn't get hurt in an accident because the boat was one big mass of people. We shot out of the slip so rapidly that everyone swayed toward the rear. I was glad to be wearing the extra padding. I could feel Susan tighten up as I attempted to hold her in my arms around the life jackets. The set of her jaw told me that she was biting her lip. It was a trick that she had learned with horses; create pain to overcome fear.

The channel to Paradise was unmarked. It was a complicated passage winding between the rocky islands, some large and some small and all dangerous. In places it was only twenty metres wide, but that didn't seem to bother our new driver. He went flat out. It was pitch black and he wasn't using a searchlight. He was running the route by memory in the dark. Occasionally, in a narrow section, a rock would flash by, dimly lit by the red running light on our side.

Susan spoke into my ear, "I wish we had never come."

"I'm sorry about that," I said, "but you got a tennis date with the blond superstar." The weak joke won a little smile.

The harrowing ride lasted twenty-five minutes. Our only problem was staying on our feet as the crowd shifted back and forth each time the boat banked into another high-speed turn. When we finally stopped at the town dock, you could hear a collective sigh of relief.

The exit ramp was near the front, so I looked to see if I knew the ace water pilot. I couldn't believe my eyes. It was Gary Pettigrew. He was relaxing with a beer. The image before me was totally out of character with the man that I knew as manager of the Airways. I stood there with my mouth open. Apparently he had started working for Bannister by driving a water taxi for several years.

He saw me and said, "I think Bannister would appreciate it if you left the life jacket on board. I mean, it looks cute on you, but I don't think you'll need it in the Volkswagen."

"Sure, Gary," I said, yanking at the straps, "thanks for the ride."

"You're welcome."

33/ THE EAGLE

The week after the party I flew on a strange type of emergency. It began with Beverly receiving a breathless phone call from the Ministry of Soil and Sea. They needed a pilot and an airplane to carry two senior naturalists north, immediately. Beverly started to tell them that we were all booked, but Pettigrew cut in on the line. He always kept his door ajar to monitor the outer office. He picked up the phone and talked over Beverley.

Flights for ministry personnel represented 25 percent of the Airways' revenue, so Gary wasn't about to disappoint anyone in their office. He told the man to come right over, slotting me in for the trip. Gary considered my students his most expendable customers, so he told Beverly to cancel my next lesson and asked Sam to ready the Found. I returned from instructing Bud Anderson and discovered two agitated passengers sitting in the Found, waiting for me. Even Sam had a hurry-up look as he helped us tie up the Supercub.

"Dad wants you to take these men up to Round Lake," Sam said, pointing north.

I told Bud that I would see him next week and asked Sam to get me some maps covering north of town. There were three Round Lakes in our vicinity.

One of the passengers yelled through the open door of the Found. "We know where it is. We must hurry so we don't miss it."

I leaned into the plane and asked, "What don't we want to miss?" I had never seen either of the gentlemen before.

"We have a report of an eagle nesting at Round Lake. If it's true, it will be the first one in this area in twelve years. Would you please hurry?"

Sam was still standing on the dock with his mouth open. I waved him off, checked the fuel quantity and climbed into the airplane.

As we taxied for takeoff, the two men explained that there was an old eagle's nest in a tree on Round Lake and someone had seen a large bird in it. They were anxious to find out if it was an eagle. They told me to fly a slow pass over it so they could take pictures, but we had to be careful not to disturb the occupant.

"And you know where the nest is located," I said. I had learned that passengers who say they know the way are telling one of the three biggest lies in bush flying. Invariably they get lost, either because time has dimmed their memories or because everything looks different from the air. (The other two passenger lies are, "Three hours without a washroom is no problem," and "I'm feeling fine.")

They said to fly north. They were familiar with the nest and could direct me to it with no problem. I continued because my student had been cancelled, I had plenty of fuel and they were paying for this trip by the hour.

I took off into the wind toward the southwest and then circled, northbound. Both men were intently watching the ground, but neither of them offered any more direction. I flew to the nearest lake that I knew as Round Lake. It was just twenty-five kilometres from town. As soon as I started circling, they each gave me a negative look. The guy sitting up front cupped his hands over my ear and yelled, "This isn't Round Lake."

I shrugged my shoulders and extended my open hand as an offer. It was their turn to find a Round Lake.

The man next to me yelled, "Ardbeg."

Ardbeg was a maintenance stop on the rail line twenty kilometres further north. It was abandoned, but fishermen still got off the train there on the way to nearby Wahwashkesh Lodge. I knew of no Round Lake in that area, but I went there anyway. When we arrived, my two navigators stared at me like we were lost and it was my fault. Their problem was that a lake visited every twelve years looks a lot different on an office wall map than it does from a speeding Found.

I indicated that I would circle the area. I flew increasingly larger rings to the right with them scanning miles of water and trees. I could tell by their colour that their excitement was turning to frustrated anger. After thirty minutes I was about to suggest that we go back for a chart, when they found it. It wasn't Round Lake; it was a tiny unnamed round lake that was really just a high-water swamp filled with tree stumps. There was a huge bird's nest in the skeleton of a tree standing near the shore.

I swung the Found around for the low pass, slowing down to 150 kilometres per hour. I needed full RPM on the propellor governor to maintain the speed with the flaps down. As the prop wound up, shock waves from the blade tips reverberated off the floats, like the sound of a hundred machine guns shooting into empty steel barrels. If we weren't going to disturb the bird, we should have been in a different county.

I flew the pass a half-kilometre away from the nest. One naturalist took pictures from the front seat while the other panned with binoculars. I pulled up and looked at them to see how they had made out. Not well. We had been travelling at forty metres per second and I doubt either one of them saw the lake in their viewfinders. They gestured that we had to fly another pass, closer.

This time I passed the nest about two hundred metres away. It was a hot, bumpy afternoon. For my passengers, it must have been like trying to take a picture of a face in a crowd while riding sideways on a runaway merry-go-round. I pulled up, and they signalled for another pass, closer.

By now I figured that a bird with any sense would be well on his way back to the continental divide or wherever eagles come from, but these men were the naturalists. I arranged our next attack to pass within fifty metres of the nest. This time, over the snarl of the propellor, I could hear the camera and binoculars hitting the plexiglass windows as both men scrambled to focus on the tree top. The fact that we were flying closer at the same speed gave them less time to see anything. But this time the guy in the back got excited. He had spotted a bird. We had to fly closer so he could see if it was an eagle.

The man beside me cupped my ear again and yelled, "Closer, but don't disturb it."

Certainly. Any bird still there would be less disturbed by a ground team dynamiting the tree. I gestured to the naturalist in the back to put down his binoculars. On this next overflight, I was going to make sure that he could see the fleas on the bird without the glasses, if eagles had fleas. He understood.

I set up the run in a level sideslip to the right. I put the nest between the right wing tip and the right float of the Found and hit full throttle. As we flashed past, I looked out the side window between my passengers and caught a glimpse of the bird on the other side of the airplane. It was an egret, the only large bird dumb enough to stand up to a charging Found. That millisecond view of him was frozen on my mind. The look on his face was more curiousity than surprise, as if he were pleased that we had finally come close enough so he could see who we were!

34/ A PILOT'S AIRPLANE

The sign was written in hand-lettered capitals and posted on the notice board at the Sturgeon Bay Marina gas shack:

SIGHTSEEING FLIGHTS—SUNDAY
1:00 PM—MARINA—$5

I was standing beside it, killing my thirst with a pop. Besides being parched, I was tired, sore and extremely happy. The poster was the cause of my fatigue and my satisfaction. I had just taken 104 people for ten-minute sightseeing flights in the Beaver, six at a time.

Sightseeing flights were a Sunday ritual at the Airways. Each week, one of our Beaver pilots visited an area marina or provincial park. It was a good business. Each place would advertise for us in advance, happy to have the extra activity at their establishment. We kept all the money; cash, no receipts. Just the thought of it made Pettigrew's eyes dance.

Fortunately for me, the repetition of the short hops had worn thin with the other pilots. Henry had grown tired of them by May 1, 1952. Jake lasted until June '72. That's when he let a pretty girl ride up front with him. Too much sun, too much excitement, too much lunch and too much turbulence; it had added up to too much. It wouldn't have been so bad if Jake hadn't used a steep bank to the left so his passenger would lean over him to see out his window.

"It was awful, believe me." Jake said.

I believed him, but the Beaver was a thoroughbred bushplane and I longed to fly it. I had spent most of the summer flogging the reluctant Found with one or two passengers, while watching the other pilots load four men and a week's worth of gear in the Beaver, tie a canoe onto the outside and take off in a third the distance.

After Jake's "never again" sightseeing flight, Len Willard was checked out on the Beaver for the job. He lasted until August before he told Pettigrew that he needed Sundays off to visit his girlfriend in Orillia. Jake said that Len made the mistake of telling his honey about the hot bikini passengers at the provincial park, and she had put her foot down.

Henry said it was because love is thicker than money.

Whatever the reason, Henry spoke the magic words on a Sunday in August without any warning: "Do you want a checkout on the Beaver?"

"Yes sir, anytime," was my immediate reply.

"Now. And when we're done, you can fly the Sturgeon Bay barf hops this afternoon."

"Yes sir." You could have flown a Beaver through my grin.

When Henry went over the pre-flight inspection with me, it was obvious that he loved the airplane. He gently touched each part as he explained its function. There was no throttle-jamming or door-slamming when Henry flew the Beaver; every movement was easy and deliberate.

"You have to treat this airplane like a woman," Henry said. "If you try and control her, she'll take over. You just guide her along with a firm hand and let her think she is in command."

The Beaver was designed and manufactured in Canada during the 'fifties and 'sixties by the DeHavilland Aircraft Company. Its features were large doors and a flat floor for easy loading, belly fuel tanks for a low centre of gravity and a cockpit-mounted oil-filler tube for long flights. Best of all, it was a friendly airplane. Just sitting in it made me feel good. Like all bush planes, its paint was chipped and it smelled of a thousand dead fish, but the Beaver had a solid warmth to it. It was a big airplane, but it didn't have the anvil disposition of the Found or the fragile flimsiness of the Cessna.

The Beaver was a pilot's airplane built for the bush. If you did everything right, it rewarded you with performance that beat all airplanes, including the lightweight Supercub. Its starting sequence made the pilot look like an orchestra conductor. He set the mixture to idle cut-off, the prop to full fine and the throttle to one-third on the centre power console. His right hand moved to the lever between the seats to pump up the fuel pressure, five pumps; his left hand reached down to the floor by the pilot's door to prime, two strokes for a cold start on a warm day. He left the primer up and used that hand to engage the starter. After three blades, he continued cranking, while hitting the magneto ignition switches. When the engine fired, he moved the mixture to auto rich with his right hand and smoothly injected the last stroke of prime with his left, while adjusting the throttle down with his right.

The Pratt and Whitney radial would pop, first on one cylinder and then on several more. With pauses in between, the pops would finally settle down to the throaty, rhythmic sequence of firing that is peculiar to radial engines.

Henry made me repeat the starting ritual several times while still tied to the dock. If the procedure was executed in the right order, the engine always ran, but if there was any variation, you could crank all day to no avail, if the battery would let you.

When we finally moved out, Henry didn't display any of the anxiety of my previous checkouts. There was only one control wheel in the airplane, but this time he was relaxed. I soon discovered that the Beaver was so docile he never felt that a new pilot could get too far behind the airplane.

With just two of us on board, the take-off run was short. I could feel the power of the 450 horses accelerating the big airplane, but I was sitting up so high that it felt like we were barely moving when the Beaver mounted the step. Then without rotating, the airplane just popped into the air in a level attitude.

We flew a few circuits, and I had the same feeling on the approach. It looked like we weren't moving. We weren't. When landing with flaps extended, the ailerons dropped as well. We were approaching into a good wind, and the Beaver just hung in the air like a two-ton kite. It was a pussycat.

When the checkout was finished, I headed for Sturgeon Bay Marina and my 104 customers. I loaded all the green-looking pretty girls in the back and kept the turns to a minimum. I felt more and more comfortable with the airplane with each hop. When I was done, I didn't care if I ever did another sightseeing flight, but I didn't want to fly any other airplane.

35/ IT'S A LONG WAY TO TOBERMORY

The nearest aviation weathercrew was stationed at Muskoka, seventy-five kilometres to the southeast. We never called them. Henry didn't believe they could know about the weather coming to Paradise. They had been wrong before and they would be wrong again. As Henry said, "Once bitten, twice cured. I don't need them fellas to look outside for me."

He was right, of course. Twenty-five years of flying from one base should have left him with a good idea of the local weather. So I asked him what I should expect on my charter to Tobermory. It looked fine; the day had dawned beautifully clear and calm, but he liked being asked.

"It's going to blow like a fart in a beer mug, but you'll be all right if you take lots of gas and land in the lee," he said.

The bay was smooth as a mirror and the windsock was hanging straight down, so I challenged him. "How do you know it's going to be windy?"

"I spotted a rooster tying himself to a three-furrow plough on my way to work this morning," he said with a smile.

I knew that Henry believed most old wives' tales and his permanent grin made it hard to tell if he was kidding. I looked at him sideways.

"I'm just joshing," he said. "When I preflighted the Beaver, I saw the altimeter setting was up almost an inch from last night. Changing pressure that fast is like stepping on a cooked onion. It's going to blow."

Henry was accurate as usual; I did make out all right, but the wind made the flight uncomfortable for my passenger.

Tobermory was due west of Paradise, 120 kilometres across the middle of Georgian Bay. It was a small town perched on the tip of the Bruce Peninsula. The Bruce stuck into Lake Huron like a rude finger, forming the southern half of Georgian Bay. Tobermory had two reasons to exist; it was the southern terminal for the car/truck ferry that ran up to Manitoulin Island and it was the scuba diving capital of the east. The exceptionally clear waters around Tobermory contained many shipwrecks, a legacy from the days when wooden ships were the backbone of eastern Canada's transportation. The area was a diver's paradise.

My passenger for this trip was Jack VanSickle. He was a young sailor from the Canada Coast Guard vessel *Griffin*. When it docked at Paradise, Jack received a four-day pass to see his girlfriend in Tobermory. Using public transport would have meant taking the bus via Toronto, a two-day trip each way, so he came to the Airways. The bus may have been faster.

Our cheapest transport was the Supercub, at twenty cents a kilometre. The trip still cost him over $96, because it was company policy to measure mileage around the shoreline of Georgian Bay. In this case, that doubled the distance, and we charged for both ways.

It was also company policy that we fly the shoreline, so in the event of an engine failure we didn't have to land in the middle of nowhere. It was a sensible rule, since the chances of a small floatplane surviving a landing in the large swells that built up across the open water were slim.

Henry's predicted wind was picking up as Jack and I lifted off at ten o'clock. The winds aloft were already strong, blowing from the west. We headed south in the Supercub, and I had to crab to the right so much that we were going sideways over the ground. I did a ground speed check and got fifty knots. That meant two hours and twenty-five minutes to Tobermory; not bad. Jack would be a little late for his luncheon date with his girl, but the flight was smooth, and he seemed to enjoy watching the scenery slowly slide by.

An hour later we turned west at Wasaga Beach and stopped moving forward. We were still flying through the air, but not over the ground. We were headed into the teeth of the wind. The smooth air also stopped. The wind was now blowing from the Blue Mountains and it was turbulent. We bounced helplessly in place, while the trucks on Highway 26 passed us.

I dropped down low where the wind was usually lighter. The turbulence was worse, but it looked like we were going a little faster, if only because we were closer to the ground. When a Volkswagon pulling a house trailer passed us, I figured we were doing thirty-five knots. That meant two hours and ten minutes to Tobermory from there. The Cub carried four and a half hours' fuel so we had plenty of gas. Jack seemed engrossed with the close-up view of the shoreline, so I dismissed any idea of turning back and refunding his money. We would be okay if the wind didn't get any stronger.

It did. Two hours from Paradise, we turned up the Bruce Peninsula by Meaford. We were now exposed to the wind blowing unchecked across 160 kilometres of Lake Huron, stronger and more turbulent than ever. Jack's pallid face wasn't looking down any more. He was staring straight ahead, probably wishing he had hitchhiked. I felt badly that he had paid so much money to endure this long confinement in the bucking Supercub. It took us ten minutes to cross the eight kilometres at the mouth of Owen Sound; we were now flying at twenty-five knots over the ground.

We finally arrived at Tobermory after three hours and forty-five minutes of flying. I landed in the lee east of the point. When I opened the door, seaman Jack threw up. It took us another fifteen minutes of slow taxiing through large swells to get around to the harbour.

I pulled up to the government dock and we were greeted immediately by a short, round Canada Customs official in full uniform. He smiled and said, "Hello. Where are you from?"

"Paradise," I replied.

"What country are you citizens of?" he asked politely.

"We're both Canadians," I said.

"Do you have anything to declare?"

I was buzzed by the long flight, but at this point I realized that he thought we were in from the United States. I considered interrupting this civil servant to explain why we didn't need to clear customs, but discretion dictated otherwise. "No sir, we have nothing to declare."

"How long will you be in Canada?"

"I'm just dropping this man off for a four-day stay and I'm heading right back to Paradise."

"Very well," he said, writing something down on a clipboard, "Welcome to Tobermory."

"Thank you."

During this conversation, I noticed two girls in halter tops and short shorts bouncing up to the plane behind the customs man. It was Jack's girlfriend and a friend. He unfolded himself from the back seat and she gave him a big hug and a long kiss that must have tasted awful to her. I tied up and waited until they were finished. The other girl offered Jack a drink in a tall glass.

"I don't think I should try that just now, thanks," he said.

"Hey, what about me?" I asked, just for fun. "I did all the flying while Jack just sat in the back."

"Oh, I'm sorry," she said. She came over and surprised me with a big kiss and the drink. "Welcome to Tobermory."

I felt myself blushing. She wasn't the best looking girl in the world, but it was a nice greeting for a total stranger. No wonder the divers liked Tobermory.

I had an inspiration that I felt would help Jack get his money's worth. "Would you girls like to go for a short flight over town?" I asked.

"Sure, that would be fun," the friend said excitedly.

I bought some boat gas and took Jack's girlfriend up first. The surface wind was still strong, so I had to sail the Cub out of the harbour backwards and around the point for takeoff. The air was relatively smooth where it wasn't tripping over the peninsula. She enjoyed seeing the houses from above and waving to Jack on the dock. When we taxied over the waves after landing, she leaned forward and hung on to me from behind. Before she got out, she gave me a kiss and a "thank you."

The customs officer approached the plane. "Hello. Where are you from?" he asked.

"I am the same guy you talked to thirty minutes ago. We were just on a local flight," I replied.

"Oh yes. of course," he said. He checked the aircraft registration on the clipboard before shuffling off.

The other girl was quite excited. She hung on to me while we were sailing out of the harbour, but I made her sit back and put her seat belt on for takeoff. As soon as we were airborne, she moved forward and slid her arms around me again and nuzzled the back of my neck. I know what Jake Lewis would have done in the same situation. It would have involved finding a secluded lagoon and taking all his clothes off. But I wasn't Jake. I was still a newlywed, and the situation made me uncomfortable. She was a big girl and the thought of all that randy flesh loose in the airplane frightened me.

I tried to ignore her as we circled the town, but her fingers wandering around my waist got lower. I let go of the control stick to move her hands away. It was a mistake. With her weight forward, the airplane suddenly dropped its nose. Without her seat belt on, she was pinned against the Supercub's roof. She let out a scream that was cut off when I pulled the stick back to recover from the dive. The quick change in "g" forces slammed her into the seat.

I cut the power and dove for the lee side of the point before she could attack me in the air again. We landed, and as we taxied around to the harbour, she put her arms around me. A curious boater approached so she didn't go any farther.

"I'm going to head back to Paradise now, but I will always remember Tobermory," I said to her as we came to the dock. To sound more convincing I added, "I have more flights today and I'm already late."

As she was getting out of the back seat, she spoke straight into my ear, "Okay Loverboy, but you know that you've changed the image of bush pilots forever."

Jack came up to the Cub and held the wing for her. "Boy, you two must have been having fun up there. The airplane was all over the sky."

"Yes, I don't remember ever encountering turbulence like that before," I said. "Nice to meet you Jack. Enjoy your stay. Bye everyone."

I pushed off to their good-byes. It was close to my next booking at four o'clock, so I climbed up to three thousand metres and headed straight for Paradise across Georgian Bay. At that altitude I was able to raise Beverly on the unicom and tell her that I would be late. I justified the direct routing to myself by thinking that I could glide most of the way home with that tailwind. It was true. I covered the distance in forty minutes, averaging about one hundred knots including the long climb.

Jake would have been disappointed in my reaction to the girl's come-on, but that didn't bother me too much. I had preserved my modesty and my marriage. It may have been at the expense of the Canadian bush pilot's macho reputation, but Jake was never going to know about it.

Sam gave me a strange look when I jumped into the bay with my clothes on at the end of the day. I was trying to eliminate the perfume and lipstick residue. Thank goodness for smoky campfires and dim Colemans.

36/ HOT DOG

The only times I flew the Beaver in August were for the tourist giggle trips every Sunday. This was before campgrounds had discovered arcades, so sightseeing flights were popular. Camping parents were always desperate for something new to occupy their children, before they ripped the tent and each other apart. The passengers were usually a dad with his kids. Mom stayed grounded on the pretense that someone would have to notify the rest of the family in the event of a crash. The real reason was to get a turn enjoying ten minutes without the children.

The kids liked the flights, but not for the view. They became disoriented right after takeoff and soon lost interest in watching large quantities of unidentified water and trees. The fun part for them was discovering that they could laugh and scream in the Beaver without being heard. No one told them to be quiet, and if dad chose to ask them to sit still, they couldn't hear him.

I enjoyed the flights, even if I wasn't hauling moose quarters, drums of fuel or canoes. The airplane's uninsulated roar and sure-footed handling always made me feel like a real bush pilot.

To prevent boredom during the repeated ten-minute hops, I practised pushing the airplane to its limits. I pretended that the take-off and landing space was restricted. Imagining a wall of trees in front of me, I would haul the willing Beaver out of the water at incredibly slow speeds and short distances. On the approach, the loads of tourists would innocently wave at their friends below, while I hung the big bush plane near the stall and dropped it into the water, stopping in a few hundred metres. After several Sundays of practise, I felt confident that I could operate the airplane out of a swimming pool.

At the end of the month, I finally got my chance to fly the Beaver on a real charter. Jake and Len were both off and Henry was booked to take the Fergusons from Paradise to their cottage on Healy Lake. The Fergusons were an elderly couple who had been customers of the Airways for a long time.

Just before they were scheduled to arrive, Beverly received a phone call from Lady Cochrane in Toronto asking if Henry would be kind enough to fly down and pick her up for a run to her cottage.

Lady Cochrane was the wealthy matriarch of a Canadian department store family. Henry had been flying her clan to their summer homes among the islands near Paradise for twenty-five years. Everyone at the Airways knew that the Cochranes would rather swim than allow anyone other than Henry to fly them up north.

The Fergusons and the Cochranes always wanted a Beaver, so Henry had to decide which customer to disappoint. He thought for a moment and said, "The Fergusons booked first, so tell Lady Cochrane that she will have to wait until I do another trip."

I could tell that he didn't like jeopardizing the better revenue of the Toronto flight, but to him, fair was fair. Fair or not, Pettigrew had already made a different decision for him. He had picked up the other phone and told Lady Cochrane that Henry would be delighted to come for her and would be leaving shortly. He came out of his office and told the chief pilot exactly that.

"That isn't right," Henry said, towering over the manager, "She could have waited. Why did you do that?"

"For several reasons, Henry," Gary said, holding his ground. "Lady Cochrane spends more money here than anyone else and she is a good friend of the Bannisters. There are two Beavers and we have another pilot available to fly the other one. You go to Toronto and your sightseeing specialist here can take care of the Fergusons."

Henry and I were both surprised at Gary's sudden assertiveness. We were hearing the almighty dollar talking, but our mercenary manager had a good case this time, so Henry didn't pursue the matter any further. He left for Toronto before the Fergusons arrived at our dock. Pettigrew conveniently disappeared at the same time.

Charter flying ranks with going to a familiar hairdresser. Our regular customers all had their favorite pilots and they liked to stick with them. They hated surprise changes.

With that in mind, I approached Mr. Ferguson with a big smile and overstated confidence. When he and his wife backed their car up to our dock, I said "Good afternoon sir, I'm the pilot for your flight today."

"Where's Henry?" the little man snapped. He put more force behind the words than I thought possible for someone his age.

"He was suddenly called away on another flight," I said with much less confidence.

"Then we'll wait!" he snapped again and dismissed me by turning back to his car.

"He just left for Toronto, sir," I called after him, "But suit yourself."

He turned and eyed me up and down. "I don't like to be jerked around, sonny," he said in a slightly quieter voice.

"I know what you mean; neither do I," I said. "Henry trained me to fly this airplane and I do a good job. If you would like to wait, it's up to you." That was the extent of my salesmanship. If the gingery old man still wasn't satisfied, then he would have to wait.

"Very well, young man," he said, "We don't want to sit here all day, so we'll see how good you are. Look lively with our bags."

"Yes sir," I replied and jumped to help them unload their car.

They didn't have very much cargo, just some hand luggage and a few groceries. The whole load, Fergusons included, could have gone in the Cessna, but anyone who flew in the bush regularly would prefer the Beaver if they could afford it.

Mrs. Ferguson let me help her up the impossible step between the airplane's float and the fuselage. Mr. Ferguson wouldn't. He stubbornly struggled into the seat next to mine. I maintained a cheerful air, despite the stony looks on their faces. I was determined to show these people that they had stumbled on an ace pilot.

I did everything slowly and deliberately, just like Henry would have done. The Beaver responded in kind by starting on my first try. I checked all the controls and gauges several times and scanned the skies for traffic. I flashed them both a big smile and took off. They just sat there like they were waiting for a new dentist to perform a double root canal. I flew as smoothly as possible, never banking more than ten degrees, and headed directly for their cottage.

Henry had shown me on the office wall chart where they were going. I found the place on the first pass. Healy Lake covered a large area, but was made up of several small inlets separated by numerous peninsulas and islands. Theirs was the only cottage on a small bay at the northernmost end of the lake. I pointed to it, and Mr. Ferguson gave me an affirming nod.

The location was perfect for me to really show my stuff. I could have landed easily in the larger part of the lake and taxied around the point to their cottage, but I didn't. I knew from my sightseeing practise that I could squeeze the Beaver into their small bay instead.

I checked it out for rocks and logs and started an impossibly slow, curving descent with the flaps and ailerons fully extended. The airplane was sluggish, but with the light load, there was still some response remaining. It was an approach that felt good all the way. We skimmed over the shoreline trees with just enough room to spare and dropped onto the surface in front of their dock. The airplane glided to a stop before I needed to turn around the point for extra room. I taxied back to their place and tied up.

They seemed unmoved by my stirring performance. Neither one said anything as I helped them unload, but I knew that I must have won them over. When everything was out of the plane and we came to the time when they should have either tipped me or at least given me a big thank you, Mr. Ferguson finally spoke. "Will Henry be picking us up when we're booked out next week?" His tone was quiet, but still sharp.

"Yes sir, if you like," I replied.

"I most certainly would," he said. To answer the questioning in my voice, he added, "In all the years that Henry has been flying my wife and me to this place, he has never once been foolish enough to try and land in this bay. He always lands on the other side of the point and taxis around."

Mr. Ferguson didn't wait for my reply. I had none to give him. He picked up a bag and tottered toward the cottage. The best that I could do was humbly taxi around the point and take off from the larger part of the lake, even though I knew the empty Beaver would easily depart from their bay.

37/ Cricket

Our promised cottage was available the first week in September. It was really a small, uninsulated, clapboard shack. It was dirty and rundown, but we didn't care; it was a cabin beside a lake, a castle by our tent standards. It came with an old propane fridge and stove. The other furniture was pilot lounge vintage, but in useable condition.

Our new home was at Green Lake, twenty kilometres east of Paradise, near the sleepy hamlet of Bruinville. The cabin was owned by Dieter and Helga Reinhart, an older couple with one heavyset son still living at home. Their house and barn stood across a small pasture from us. They farmed the property part-time, cutting hay for a few cows. Their boy Adolf did the chores when the bus brought him home after high school.

Dieter Reinhart worked full time as the area's interior paint and paper man. That seemed like a joke, after seeing the ancient yellowed wallpaper and faded paint in our cabin and his own home. There was no evidence of any interior decorating having been done by anyone for generations. But he did go somewhere every weekday morning.

The only exceptional thing about the whole family was their car. It was a red 1957 Mercedes-Benz diesel, the only one within a hundred miles and the pride of the family. Every morning Dieter washed it before driving off to a job.

They were nice people, but it was a mistake to engage them in conversation, unless you had a lot of time and nothing to do. They loved to talk, but they had nothing to say.

"Good evening Mrs. Reinhart, I brought you the money for our propane."

"Come in, come in. Would you like a cup of tea?"

"Yes, thank you. It has been a beautiful day, hasn't it?" I replied.

"Ja, ja, it has been a beautiful day. Dieter don't you think it has been a beautiful day?" she would say.

"Ja, ja, it has been a beautiful day, that's for sure." Dieter would answer from a stuffed chair near the kitchen stove.

"Adolf, don't you think it has been a beautiful day?" Mrs. Reinhart would say. Adolf was always eating something at the kitchen table.

"Ja," Adolf would answer with his mouth full.

Then Dieter would remember there was something that he had forgotten to mention. "Of course, yesterday was a beautiful day, Ja?"

"Ja, yesterday was a beautiful day," Mrs. Reinhart would reply. "Adolf, yesterday was a beautiful day, Ja?"

"Ja."

If the conversation didn't kill you, the tea would. It came from a pot on their propane stove. Every morning, they added tea leaves and water to whatever was in there from the night before. The burner was always on. When the pot got low, they added more. I doubt they ever dumped it out except into my cup. They didn't use a strainer and it plopped more than poured. I knew the mixture was eating the pot because I could taste the steel when I took a sip.

It was obvious after one cool night that the cottage would not do us for the winter. Turning on the stove for warmth heated the whole county. The clapboard was nailed to the two-by-four frame and that was it. I could see that when the snow started flying in November, it would blow right in. But the rent was free, and for the time being Green Lake was better than the tent.

Soon after we moved in, Susan made an announcement. She saw the cottage as an opportunity to fulfill her lifelong dream. One night after a macaroni and cheese supper cooked on a real stove, she said, "Pamela Mason is going to sell some of the horses, instead of feeding them all winter."

"Sounds smart to me," I replied, vainly trying to find better accommodation in the *Bannister Bugle.*

"This time of year they will only go for meat," she continued.

"Someone has to feed the dogs of the world," I said. We had not been married a full year, but I was catching on. Susan loved animals and wanted a horse.

"Pamela said that I could have Cricket in exchange for our tent. She would like to see Cricket go to a good home rather than for meat."

I put the paper down. "Our beloved tent? I was thinking that we could raise it in here so we don't freeze over the winter." I was kidding and she knew it.

"They have an English saddle and bridle that they will give me for $100." She was watching me closely.

I suppose it was a fair deal. A "free" horse and an old English saddle that the Masons couldn't use in exchange for a month of Susan's wages and a tent with black mold growing up the inside.

"Did you talk to the Reinharts about using an empty stall in their barn?"

"Yes!" she said with mounting excitement, "You won't regret this, believe me. I'll take good care of her and let you ride her whenever you want."

She was bursting with pleasure. She jumped in my lap and gave me a big hug. It was like Christmas and a honeymoon combined. I said yes to the horse and won big brownie points that lasted for weeks.

Cricket was probably the worst animal that Susan could have found, but you can't tell that to a girl about her first horse. It would not have mattered if Cricket had had two heads and only one leg, she was Susan's to have and to hold and nothing could diminish that.

Cricket was an ex-rodeo horse whose years of barrel racing had left her with a hard mouth and a set mind. She had one speed and that was flat out. She didn't stop until she reached her stall. Cricket had cleaned off a few tourists at the barn door before the Masons discovered what they had purchased. They reserved her for the few local cowboys who knew how to ride and loved to let her run. By the end of the summer, she was skinny and miserable. Pamela Mason probably could not have sold her for dog food because there wasn't enough meat left on her bones.

Susan bought hay and straw from the Reinharts and made a bed more lavish than the horse had seen all her life. When the Masons delivered her by trailer, she settled into her new home like she had deserved it all along.

There was an abandoned railway line running through the bush near our cabin. The tracks were removed, making it an ideal riding path. Cricket would walk nicely for Susan as far as she wanted to go up the trail, but, when they turned around, she would explode into a flat-out run for the barn. No amount of pulling on the reins or beating her over the head with a crop would slow her down. A summer's riding had left Susan fit and experienced enough to be able to stay on the speeding horse when they were going straight, but Cricket wasn't very smart. She would forget which turnoff led back to the farm. If they passed an opening in the bush at a full gallop and Cricket decided it might be the right one, she would suddenly plant her front feet and pivot around. She would make the turn without slowing down. The manoeuvre launched Susan every time.

Cricket always made it home first. When I saw her crossing the pasture to the barn, it was my cue to drive the Volkswagen up the line. I would find Susan limping back with her helmet in her hand and our dog Lady at her side.

The horse should have gone for glue, but Susan was determined that the tender loving care and training she heaped on Cricket would make her behave. The horse seemed adamant to prove her wrong, subscribing to the theory "once a knothead, always a knothead." They made a good pair; the horse never learned and Susan never stopped trying.

38/ SILVER RIVER

The pace at the Airways changed in September. There were no more sightseeing flights or floatplane checkouts. The steady flow of summer tourists ended on Labour Day. The whole town seemed to breathe a collective sigh of relief as if a weight had been lifted from its shoulders. The line of people outside the ice cream parlor was gone, and I could get service in the Canadian Tire store. The cottagers, the Ministry of Soil and Sea, student pilots, and fishermen continued to use the Airways, but the rush of squeezing in that extra flight ended. Even Pettigrew seemed to relax a little.

Len Willard went back to school as planned. He enrolled in a business course at a community college, hoping it would better his chances of being hired by the airlines. We had a party with our beer bottle money in his honour at the Queens. Jake told Len that he would be back next year, because the college would make him too smart and the airlines wouldn't take him. Len just smiled and said nothing. I never saw him again.

Pettigrew told me that there would be an increase in student pilots after the locals had counted their money from the summer. He was wrong. By the end of September, I had only four customers learning to fly.

Henry gave me one of his mail runs. The Airways had a federal government contract to fly the mail twice a week to Silver River and Carefree. This sounds good, but it requires a little explanation. The Silver River post office was only twenty-five kilometres south of Paradise, in a local marina's general store. Carefree was also just a marina with a tuck shop. It was located twelve kilometres west of Silver River on the last row of islands before the open waters of Georgian Bay. The entire round-trip triangle used up about twenty minutes flying time in the Cessna 180. It was true that both spots were inaccessible by road, but the run could have been done with a boat in half a day. Bannister made sure that Pettigrew underbid the water taxis because the run constituted a scheduled air service. The plane departed every Tuesday and Thursday at ten o'clock. That meant the Airways qualified as a scheduled airline, and as president, Bannister could then fly standby with his family on any other airline in the world for a 10 percent fare, which he often did when he took holidays.

Henry always looked forward to the flights and usually milked them for two hours. I was surprised when he announced that he was taking Tuesday off and asked me to fly the mail for him. I didn't mind because it was something different to do.

The two post offices were maintained for the convenience of the local cottagers. After Labour Day, the bags became pitifully light, but I obediently loaded them into the Cessna without saying anything. The first stop was Silver River where the post office/general store was run by a kindly widow named Mrs. Beamer. She was a tall, thin lady in her fifties. Her hair was mostly silver, and she was neatly dressed in flannel slacks and a lacey blouse with a white sweater draped over her shoulders. She looked smart with her bit of make-up, but her expression was sad.

"Hi," I said, walking in the door. "I'm the mailman today. How are you?"

"I'm fine, thank you," she replied a bit weakly. "I'm Mrs. Beamer; pleased to meet you."

I introduced myself and looked around while she emptied the sack and put the return mail in it.

"Where is Henry today?" she asked.

"He took a day off and asked me to do this run," I replied.

The shop was unusually neat for a country store. I could see through a door behind the counter into the tidy living quarters. A table was set for two on a pretty lace cloth.

"I don't recall Henry ever taking a Tuesday off before," she said.

"No, me either," I answered. "I think he is catching up on a few missed days from the summer."

"I suppose," she said.

"Well, nice talking to you Mrs. Beamer. No doubt Henry will be back on this run Thursday. Bye for now."

"Goodbye," she said, smiling a little more.

The girl at the Carefree post office was more my speed. Angela was the twenty-year-old wife of the marina manager. I had met her before on charter flights to the island. She was a bright, cheerful kind of girl who always made you feel welcome.

"Hi there. I see you've been promoted to mailman," she said with a big smile. "Did the bags get too heavy for old Henry?"

"No, he just took a day off. How are you? Are you still saving up for flying lessons?" I asked.

"I sure am, but it's a slow process working here. I don't think you will see me in that pilot seat for a while."

"Well, keep counting those pennies."

"Okay. Here you go," she said, handing me the bag.

I was back at the Airways in an hour. There wasn't much to the run, but it was a pleasant diversion. I couldn't help thinking about the contrasting female storekeepers"one happy, one sad"but they were both nice in their own ways.

On Thursday, Henry asked me if I wanted to do the mail run again.

"Sure, but you don't have to give it to me. I still fly enough with Len gone."

"Well, you go ahead this time, and I'll do the aircraft log books. We have to keep the paper-pushing government happy."

"Okay," I said.

Mrs. Beamer was neatly dressed and tastefully made-up again, but she still looked unhappy. Her voice wavered a bit when she asked where Henry was.

"He is getting caught up on some paperwork this time. Nothing important, but he asked me to do this flight again."

"Oh," was all she said.

I bid her good-bye and was secretly thankful to leave. I was glad not to be stuck in a job like hers. On my way to Carefree, I had the first germ of an idea about Mrs. Beamer. Was it possible that she had a passion for Henry, in her own way? Henry was married and had been since coming to Paradise. Maybe it was getting a little too friendly for him at Silver River? I didn't think about it much, but I was curious to see who was going to fly the mail on Tuesday.

Sure enough, he took Tuesday off and I did the mail. It looked like Mrs. Beamer was ready for him again and was clearly unhappy. She didn't say much and her hands were shaking when she put the letters in the bag. The table in the back was set for two, and I knew the second place wasn't for me.

I was in a dilemma. I didn't like being used as a solution to Henry's problem, but I couldn't discuss it with anyone at the Airways. Jake was as sensitive as a two-by-four when it came to human relations and telling Pettigrew would be like mounting loudspeakers on a truck and driving up Main Street. Susan didn't know how to be devious, so when I discussed it with her, she suggested confronting Henry straight out. I did.

When Henry and I were in the pilot shack together on Wednesday, I said, "Who is going to do the mail run tomorrow?"

"You can if you like," he replied.

"Bud Anderson may want to fly at the same time," I said.

"Well, I'm sure Bud could come before or after the mail."

His smiling face didn't give anything away, so I took a deep breath and jumped right in. "I bet Mrs. Beamer would rather you took the mail."

He looked startled. His face turned scarlet. "Since when did Mrs. Beamer have anything to say about who flies the mail?"

"She doesn't, but she seems adult enough to understand an expla-nation. If I'm wrong, tell me and I'll fly the mail tomorrow; if I'm right, you do it."

He looked me straight in the eye, long and hard. I didn't flinch but my legs went rubbery. I was beginning to think that I had stepped way out of line this time and wished I hadn't said anything.

Henry finally replied, "You may be too smart for your own britches."

"Maybe, but I trust you'll tell me if I am."

"I'll do the mail tomorrow," he said.

"Thanks Henry."

The fact that he never let the confrontation ruin our friendship was an indication of the depth of Henry's character. He did the run the next day and many after that, but he was only gone an hour each time.

39/ THE CHIEF

Ben Norton did the impossible. He flew over the Airways office and knocked down our HF radio antenna. It wasn't the antenna itself that made the feat seem impossible, it was the massive steel railway bridge that ran behind it.

The railway bridge was the highest obstruction in town. It ran less than two hundred metres behind the Airways complex and stood well above it, carrying the rails over the waterfront of Paradise. The antenna was just a tall, crooked piece of aluminum that Ken Noonan had made from scrapped TV aerials and erected on the office roof. It was held in place with liberal amounts of stovepipe wire running to the hangar and the pilot shack.

Airplanes landing from the north had to clear the railway bridge on the descent to the harbour. The Airways pilots never worried about the antenna because we cleared it if we cleared the bridge, but we always came close. The lower we approached, the less we had to taxi back to the dock.

Norton must have descended almost vertically from the bridge to hit the antenna. I didn't see him do it, but I heard the crashing aluminum from inside the office. I looked out in time to see Norton's Aeronca Chief splash into the bay, not far beyond our dock. It wasn't a bad landing by Norton's standards, a little heavy, but the airplane wasn't damaged.

The noise made Beverly duck, but it scared Pettigrew more. He came out of his office covered in milk from his chin to his knees. His eyes were bugged out, and he was still holding the empty glass.

"What was that?" he exclaimed.

"Ben Norton just arrived," I replied.

"Did he hit the roof?" Pettigrew asked.

"It sounded like it," I said as I followed him outside.

There was stovepipe wire everywhere. It was impossible to walk to the dock without getting tangled. We picked our way through while Norton taxied up, grinning. Ken and Chico joined us from the hangar.

"I guess I cut that one a little close," Norton said as he climbed from the Chief. When he saw Pettigrew, he started to laugh. Between guffaws he said, "Hey Gary; let me take you home to meet my cat. He needs a drinking buddy. Ha, ha, ha."

Ben Norton owned the excavating company in town. He was a roly-poly, easy-going guy who didn't have a serious bone in his body. He lived to laugh and laugh he did.

"I'll send you a bill for the antenna," Gary said as sternly as he could. He turned back toward the office and walked into a guy wire.

"Don't forget to charge me for the cream," Norton called after him, still laughing.

Ben Norton had learned to fly at the Airways the year before. I had met him in August when he had arrived for gas, having just purchased the Chief. At that time, he hadn't flown for a year and his dangerous arrival proved it. I didn't know him then, so I didn't offer any dual instruction. If I had, he would have declined. Norton was as stubborn as he was jolly.

It was a mistake for any novice pilot to buy a Chief on floats. The airplane was fabric-covered with high wings like the Supercub, but with two major differences: it had side by side seating which was a chummy arrangement that slowed the airplane down, and its engine was only 65 horsepower, less than half the Cub's.

Ben flew the Chief like he was still in a Supercub. When he had cleared the railway bridge, he had put the airplane in an almighty sideslip to lose altitude. The Chief was slow and lighter, so it had literally stopped moving forward and slid straight down. He was lucky that the airplane straightened out from the steep descent at such a low altitude.

The day he knocked over the antenna was only the fourth time Ben had flown the Chief. It was supposed to be the beginning of his first significant trip. Ben and an equally large buddy named Roy were loaded up for a slow northbound flight to Hearst for some moose hunting. They had stopped at the Airways for fuel.

Ken Noonan said to Ben, "Do you want me to haul her out and check for damage?"

"Naw; if she hasn't sunk by the time Sam gases her up, she'll be all right," he said with a big grin.

Beverly and I fought our way back to the office, while Ken and Chico started cleaning up the wires. We all thought that was the end of Ben Norton for the day. It nearly was.

By the time he was ready to go, the temperature had climbed considerably for a September day. It was quite noticeable because there was no wind. I was updating my student files, but I stopped to watch Ben's takeoff. The airplane seemed to struggle for a long time in the plow, but that didn't surprise me after seeing the amount of gear stuffed into it with the two men. My interest turned to concern when I saw their wake change in the distance, indicating that they were on the step. They were more than three-quarters of the way across the bay and would never make it over the trees.

I was right. They never made it into the air. Norton was still riding full power on the step when the reluctant Chief hit the far beach. I ran outside and yelled at Sam who had also been watching.

"Come on; we'll take a boat from the marina."

I sprinted across the parking lot to the Bannister Marina office. "Barry, I need the keys to the inboard/outboard; an airplane ran into the far shore."

"All right," he said slowly, and turned around to search the board that he used everyday. After checking each key, he handed one to me.

"Thar ya go."

Both Sam and Ken joined me. Ken had been smart enough to grab a fire extinguisher, first aid kit, rope and a pry bar from the hangar. I started the boat while they cast off.

As we drew closer to the Chief, we could see that it was still intact. It was parked with its nose into the trees at the end of two grooves in the sand leading from the water.

"Crazy bugger," Ken said over the noise of the boat.

Norton had been lucky, again. He had plowed into the widest stretch of beach, and the airplane had stopped just short of hitting anything solid. He and his passenger were standing beside the plane.

"I thought she was going to come off for sure. You should have seen the look on Roy's face here when we hit the beach. His eyes nearly popped right out of his head," Ben said with a laugh, slapping Roy on the shoulder. Roy grinned sheepishly and took a swig from a whiskey bottle.

With our help, Ken tipped the floats up on a log so he could check underneath. There was no damage. We unloaded the gear from inside the airplane and used Ken's rope to pull the Chief backwards off the beach with the boat. Norton was ready to try it again. He reloaded the plane and taxied around to the larger bay on the other side of Paradise. We went back to the marina, while he roared up and down the wide stretch of water for an hour. I don't think it ever occurred to Ben that there were certain conditions when a tired, old, underpowered, overloaded Aeronca Chief, flown by an idiot, would not take off.

He came back to our docks after Henry landed in the Beaver.

"Henry, old pal," he said, "I'm having trouble getting the Chief into the air. How about running the Beaver ahead of me on takeoff so I can get some extra lift?"

I stood behind Norton, shaking my head back and forth at Henry. I don't think it was necessary. He took one look at the inexperienced pilot and his buddy sucking on the whiskey bottle and said, "Not today, Ben. Some days the best way to get where you're going is to not go."

40/ MOTOR MOOSE

Toward the middle of October, the people of Paradise started gearing up for the local deer and moose hunt. It was the last kick of the cat for the tourist businesses, including the Airways. When the hunt was over, the town would virtually close up for the winter, and the unemployment office would have the biggest payroll.

Before the hunt began, I flew a head count for the Ministry of Soil and Sea. The idea of this patrol was to fly up and down the county in long narrow strips and count the deer and moose. The figures obtained helped determine the number of hunting tags that should be issued.

The same information could be obtained at the Queen's Hotel for a few beers, but not by anyone from the Soil and Sea. Many local residents had favorite hunting spots and they knew the animal population. They kept their knowledge a secret, because they regularly ignored the game laws and stocked their freezers with these animals year 'round, being careful not to wipe out the herds.

The locals all applied for resident hunting tags to prevent too many tourists from invading their territory, but they rarely hunted in the fall. They were too busy working as guides to the out-of-town hunters who did come. The guides made sure the visitors saw the smaller animals that they had selected for the hunt. This underground form of conservation had existed for generations. The Soil and Sea program was something to be tolerated and worked around without rocking the boat.

It wasn't my job to count the deer and moose. I just flew the plane, and the senior naturalist from the Soil and Sea did the counting. His name was Harvey Pendleton, and he introduced himself as "Mr.Pendleton." He was a tall, thin man whose short, grey hair was in a 'fifties brushcut. It was possible that the aerial count was initiated by Pendleton as a method of getting out of the office to enjoy the last days of good weather before winter.

On our first flight, the weather was clear and the bright sunshine set the forest's fall colors ablaze. We took the Found, since we wouldn't be landing anywhere but at the base. As we started northbound along the shore of Georgian Bay, I thought our chances of spotting anything through the colored leaves at two hundred kilometres per hour seemed remote. I was afraid that we would be reporting no animals at all and the hunting season would be closed, but Pendleton had done this before. He marked "finds" on his clipboard when I saw nothing. I watched his eyes and saw that he looked well ahead at clearings and shorelines, where the high-pitched snarl of the Found caused a head to raise or a tail to flick.

At the top of our county-long run, we flew inland a kilometre and then turned south, parallel to our original track. When we passed over an old logging road, I spotted a cow moose trotting purposefully eastward. Pendleton marked her down. The moose made good progress and on our next run north, we flew over her again. Pendleton added her to his list.

I leaned over and shouted, "We saw her before."

He frowned at me without saying anything and went back to spotting, without altering his count.

She was there again on our next leg, and Pendleton marked her a third time. Moose are not normally energetic, but this one continued to truck her way east. He counted her twice more before I worked up the courage to speak again.

"You've counted the same moose five times," I yelled in his ear.

"You fly the plane, I'll count," he shouted back. The nasty look on his face ended the conversation.

Instead of no sightings, now I was afraid that motor moose might be responsible for a high count and a tag issue that would decimate the species in the area. When we approached her again, I banked the Found slightly so Pendleton might not see her, but I wasn't quick enough. He marked her down again.

Pendleton counted her twice more before a lake forced the road and the moose to turn south. I should have said something more about her after we landed, but Pendleton's grim face intimidated me. So much for the accuracy of scientific research. I soon forgot the incident.

Two weeks later, Oscar Fleming, the cable TV man, burst into the Airways and said, "You have to get down to the Soil and Sea Office right away and buy a moose tag."

"Oscar, why do I want a moose tag?" I asked.

"Because old man Pendleton went berserk on his moose count. You must have flown him in circles over their feeding grounds. He raised the tag issue by 30 percent, and there aren't enough animals to go around."

"I didn't fly him in circles, but I can explain the high count."

"It doesn't matter now. What we need is enough residents like you to buy tags so there aren't too many left for the tourists to wipe out the herd. The deadline is 4:30 this afternoon. I have to run and get Long Sing to buy one."

I went to the Soil and Sea Office and purchased a tag. In those days the tags were not expensive, so the money wasn't important. What bothered me was that I thought I'd made it as a bush pilot in Paradise, but the locals classified me as an outsider in the same category as an eighty-year-old Chinese laundry man.

41/ FLY YELLOW SIDE UP

Pettigrew continued to assure me that the Airways would be busy enough to keep me working all winter. It was as if his own future was at stake in maintaining a flying staff. At the end of the hunting season in November, Jake Lewis would be moving back to Barrie to spend the winter driving a cab and pocketing unemployment insurance. Henry and I would be the only pilots, but I would fly with all the students.

I didn't see how it would work. I was only paid when I flew. Even with more students, there would be a limit on my income imposed by the winter's short daylight and frequent bad weather. I would lose a month's flying during the fall freeze-up and again in the spring thaw. Susan and I needed better accommodation, which was certainly going to cost more. She was only working weekends now and that would end after Thanksgiving. It didn't add up.

On the plus side, we had made some great friends. We loved being surrounded by some of the prettiest country in Canada and had come to enjoy the easy pace of living in a small town. Susan and I talked several evenings away, discussing how we might be able to stay. We knew our situation would have to change when the hunting season ended, with the onslaught of cold weather. In the end, Bannister made the decision for us.

I was talking to Pettigrew about advertising for more students when Bannister burst into the office. "What are you doing with him for the winter?" he boomed, pointing a stubby finger at me.

"We were just discussing how we might get more students," Pettigrew replied. He looked worried.

"Forget it. The locals are too tight with their money. If he stays, we have to find him something else to do. We can't have him stealing all Henry's flights. Right?"

"Right sir," Pettigrew mumbled.

It was news to me that there was any discussion of my not staying. Pettigrew had been treating me like he was afraid I would leave.

"Tell me son," the bulky owner said, turning to me, "Have you ever driven a school bus?"

"No sir," I replied. I would have said no even if I had. I didn't want to drive a school bus.

"Do you know anything about propane?" he asked hopefully.

I realized that, in his own way, he was trying to be helpful and slot me into another job for the winter, but I didn't come to Paradise to do anything but fly.

"No sir," I replied truthfully.

"Have you ever driven a snow plow?" I could tell that he was getting a little frustrated.

"No sir."

"Well damn it, boy; have you ever shovelled snow?"

"Yes sir, twice."

He missed the sarcasm in my reply. "Well that's it. You can ride as a wingman in the snowplows with Ken and Chico."

With that settled, he stormed out to bully another part of his empire. Pettigrew didn't wait to see my reaction. He went straight to the fridge for a glass of milk and then hid in his office.

As much as I liked living in Paradise, I didn't want to ride up and down the Trans Canada Highway in bad weather as a copilot in a Sicard. Bannister's manipulations forced me to decide that it was time to leave.

That night Susan and I agreed that I should look for another job somewhere in Southern Ontario. At that time of year the only flying work available was instructing. I would be going back to teaching kamikaze doctors and dentists. I didn't mind the thought if it was only for the winter. The next problem was to find the flying schools that needed pilots. I knew that my old job at home had been filled, so I had to look elsewhere.

In the meantime, I still wanted to fly at the Airways, so I had to sneak away and use the phone booth beside the ice cream parlor. Much as I hated to call him, I realized my best contact was mean old Inspector Kennedy who did flight tests all around the area. He would know about any instructor openings. I phoned his office.

"Hello, Inspector Kennedy?"

"Yes."

I could hear the granite in his voice.

"Hi. I'm the instructor from Paradise. I'm looking for another job. I was wondering if you knew of any openings around?"

There was a long silence. I knew he might have trouble placing me, but after a while I wondered if he had hung up. I was about to ask if he was still there when he said, "Job placement is not something that we do at the Department of Transport."

"I realize that, sir. I'm not looking for a recommendation; I just thought you might suggest some likely schools for me to call."

"No."

I got the message. I guess he remembered when Buttonville

Tower had questioned his ability during my flight test. It had been my fault, but I was counting on him forgetting about it.

That night I went home with an empty, unwanted feeling. In contrast, Susan was all smiles.

"I have news," she said.

"It must be better than my news."

"I phoned my old boss, Hymie Waumbaum, and told him I was looking for work. He didn't have anything, but he recommended me to a friend who is expanding a ladies' wear business in Pleasantville."

"That's great," I said, injecting some artificial enthusiasm for her sake. "Are you going to call the man?"

"I did." She was giving me a searching look.

"What did the man say?" I asked. I could tell that she was up to something.

"He offered me a job as assistant manager of a branch store in a new plaza on the edge of town."

"What did you tell the man?" The look in her eye told me to ask that question.

"Well, he needed to know right away because they're opening the store next week for the beginning of the Christmas shopping."

"What did you tell the man, Honey?"

"I told him that I would take the job," she said quietly, and then quickly added, "but I could call him back if we change my mind."

My initial reaction was anger, but I didn't let it out. She shouldn't have gone so far without consulting me. Then I remembered that I had set a precedent in that department.

Pleasantville was a small town south of London, Ontario, near Lake Erie. The population of 20,000 people supported some manufacturing, but mostly it served the rich agricultural land in the area.

"What will I do in Pleasantville?" I mumbled.

"They have a flying school; I already asked."

"The chance of them needing an instructor in a town that size is remote."

"London is nearby. That airport may have something for you."

"It might not." The conversation was bogging down, and it was my fault.

Susan took charge, "My pay will be good; I suggest that we go there for the winter. If you can't find any flying in that area by next spring, then we can move up north again."

I didn't need to see the get-me-out-of-here look on her face to know that she was right.

"Okay. You've got yourself a deal," I said, resigning myself to her logic. "Maybe Lady and I will find a stable in Pleasantville that will let us clean stalls for $5 a day."

"Sure," she said, giving me a big smile and a hug, "I could recommend you."

Susan had agreed to start her new job the following Monday. Since we just had one car, I used that excuse to quit the Airways and go with her that weekend. It meant giving Pettigrew only four days notice, but I wasn't flying much. Despite the large issue of moose tags, the hunting season had not generated much business. The Paradise area was becoming too civilized, and many hunters were travelling farther up north. I knew it wouldn't make a lot of difference if I left early.

Pettigrew took it well. "After our conversation with Bannister, I'm not surprised," he said.

I couldn't help thinking that Gary might end up riding as wingman on the snowplows in my place, but I didn't say anything about it.

I went to the pilot shack to tell Henry. "Hi. I just gave Pettigrew notice that I'm leaving at the end of this week. Susan and I are moving down to Pleasantville."

There were probably a thousand other things that I should have said to the big man, but I didn't know where to start. Henry had been the mentor who was solely responsible for leading an inexperienced city-slicker flying instructor through a busy summer of bush flying with only one small scratch. His methods were different but effective. I hadn't been the first green pilot that he had wet-nursed onto floats and I wasn't going to be the last.

"It's been a great summer, Henry. I appreciated your help." It was all that I could think to say.

It must have been hard for him to watch a parade of youngsters draw from his experience and then move on, but I think from his reply that he was used to it.

"You made a good bush pilot, even if you did come dressed funny. In this business, that's all we have to say."

And that's all he said, but from Henry, I considered it a supreme compliment.

Susan arranged for the Masons to board her horse until we could find transport for the miserable nag to join us in Pleasantville. At the end of the week, we loaded everything that we owned into the back of the Volkswagen. Lady knew the signs and pressed nervously against the car, watching the space dwindle inside. We left her room on top of the pile and with her panting grin filling the rearview mirror, we drove to the Airways for our last good-byes before heading south.

It had snowed the night before. A thick wet blanket of the white stuff covered everything. When we pulled into the parking lot, Henry and Sam were standing on the Beaver, sweeping off the wing.

"You two had better watch your step," I called. "That wing will be slicker than snot on a door knob."

"Don't you worry, young fella," Henry replied. "You just keep flying yellow side up."

ABOUT THE AUTHOR

Garth Wallace switched to full-time writing in 1990 after 14,000 hours and 19 years of bush flying, instructing and corporate flying. He and his wife live near Ottawa, Ontario where he works as a publisher for the Canadian Owners and Pilots Association.